The Holy Goalie

Moderator: the official portrait

The Holy Goalie

The Very Reverend R. Leonard Small,
CBE, MA, DD

formerly Minister of St. Cuthbert's Parish
Church, Edinburgh

The Pentland Press Limited
Edinburgh · Cambridge · Durham

First published in 1993
Reprinted in 1993 by
The Pentland Press Ltd.
1 Hutton Close
South Church
Bishop Auckland
Durham

ISBN   1 85821 037 2

Typeset by Elite Typesetting Techniques, Southampton.
Printed and bound by Antony Rowe Ltd., Chippenham.

Contents

Illustrations

Foreword

by the Very Rev. David Steel, DD, Ll.D

It is an honour to have been invited to contribute a Foreword to this most interesting book, which it has been a pleasure to read. Dr Small told me that he had been urged by his family to make this record of his life and work – especially by his grandchildren who had been fascinated by the 'tales of their grandfather'.

This life began as the first-born son of a manse in North Berwick, and there is a delightful picture of a happy childhood in that seaside town at the beginning of the century, when the local population had a regular influx of visitors who spent the summer there. Was it being born and brought up within sight and sound of the sea that began his lifelong love of the sea and ships?

He went to the local school, which was also attended by a son from another North Berwick manse, Nevile Davidson, who became Moderator of the General Assembly four years before Leonard Small held that position. There must be few 300-pupil local schools in Scotland which can claim to have produced two Moderators within a five year period.

The transition from school to Edinburgh University was not easy – it seldom is – but he emerged with a 1st Class Honours Degree in Classics, while managing to find time to play for and captain the University Soccer Team, and also to play in goal for St. Bernards FC, a well-known Edinburgh team at that time. On a notable occasion he was goalkeeper for Scotland in an International Amateur Match against England. He continued to play as goalkeeper up till the early years of his ministry in Bathgate – hence the title of this autobiography.

From University he went on to study for the Ministry at New College and was licensed in St. Giles, one of the first group of students to be licensed after the 1929 Union of the United Free Church and the Church of Scotland. He then went on to study in Zurich under Emil Brunner.

With hindsight it might be said that all that had happened so far was an excellent preparation for the Ministry. As he indicates, it gradually came to him that this was his vocation, and, as one reads the account that follows, there can be no doubt that his ministry was a response to 'the divine imperative' and was greatly blessed by God.

He became minister of four very different charges: in Bathgate; Kilmarnock; Cramond on the outskirts of Edinburgh; and finally, St. Cuthbert's in the City centre. He had the good sense to become engaged to Jean before he was called to his first charge, and they began their married life in the manse at Bathgate. My wife and I met Jean for the first time when Leonard invited me to be Associate Minister with him in St. Cuthbert's, and we immediately warmed to her and became firm friends. She was his partner throughout his whole ministry, and it was with a great sense of personal loss that we learned of her death, the day after we returned from a three months visit to America. We saw the first signs of her long illness as the four of us were returning from an official visit to the Irish General Assembly; Leonard was there as Moderator, and I as his Senior Chaplain. It was the beginning of thirteen years of a painful, disabling illness, which she bore with characteristic courage.

Our association at St. Cuthbert's with both of them was a very happy experience. We had just returned from eight years in East Africa, and I welcomed the opportunity of finding out what had been happening in my home Church, and especially of sharing in the transition from the old Collegiate set-up in St. Cuthbert's to the new: Minister plus Associate. I enjoyed a most cordial relationship with one of the most distinguished ministers of our time, but I was convinced that, once the new plans were established, I ought to go, and eighteen months later I accepted a call to St. Michael's, Linlithgow.

The ministry recorded in this autobiography is astonishing in its diversity. In addition to the churches of which Leonard Small was Minister, he was also Convener in turn of no fewer than three Assembly Committees, and in 1966 he became Moderator of the General Assembly. He also served a variety of good causes too numerous to mention. He was honoured both by the Scouts and the Boys' Brigade for long service to them – a unique double. Until recently he was for many years Regional Chaplain to the Air Training Corps, and was awarded the OBE. Later he was made a CBE for public service, notably for his work as Chairman of the Parole Board.

His ministry was also international. Many in America, Canada, New Zealand, Europe, the Far East and, most of all, in Australia – the sum of his many visits there add up to over two years – will in these pages hear again the very tone and style of a man to whom the Ministry meant service to God and man. He had a unique touch. His fellow-ministers were aware of this special gift. On one occasion a group of them were being shown around an engineering works, and one of them whispered: 'Leonard, you'll not get any illustrations here.' 'Oh,' said Leonard, 'I've just got the very thing for the sermon I'm working on for next Sunday;' and he pointed to a packing-case on which was written: DEFECTIVE – RETURN TO MAKER. They had had all seen it, but he alone saw there an illustration of what the Gospel is all about. When you think about it, that is what Jesus did. He took the common things of life to illustrate the uncommon ways of God, and it was a gift that made Leonard Small such an effective servant of his Lord, not just as a preacher, but as a pastor and a person.

I am confident that this book will be widely read and enjoyed by many throughout the world, who will recognise in the autobiography that the style is the man.

Preface

A book with such a 'way-out' title as this obviously requires some explanation, if not apology! From the age of 15 to around 26 I played football in the position of goalkeeper. At school I played in the morning for the school, and in the afternoon for the town team; at University I played for and captained the team; while at New College I played as an amateur in a professional team, St Bernard's FC in the 2nd Division of the Scottish League, and in 1929 played for Scotland in an Amateur International against England. Over the years this still keeps cropping up, and there are sections of the populace, not only the 'man in the street', but also the 'man in the pew' to whom clearly I have never done anything else that matters! Not long ago, when visiting a ward in the Royal Edinburgh Hospital, I approached a group of confused elderly men, all sitting more or less comatose. I asked, generally, if anyone could tell me where to find Mr X, the patient I was trying to visit. One of the group looked up with sudden excited interest, and, pointing to me, exclaimed: 'Here! You're the chap who used to play for St Bernard's'. When I came to live in my present retirement house my neighbour across the road, Mrs Alistair McKinlay, told me that one of her sons, having been told who was moving in across the road, reacted: 'Oh! the holy goalie!' After the choice of title had been made and the work was proceeding the same lady handed me a cutting from The Guardian, which stated, under the title 'Holy Goalies' that the Pope had been a goalkeeper and so had Cardinal Hume! This seemed to suggest it might not be such a bad idea to have the Protestant Team represented.

For the sake of brevity I'm including here my sincere thanks to those who have made this effort possible. When I was thinking about the best method of producing such a work a word processor was suggested. Now, I am scared stiff of modern technology in any such form, but I was vastly aided, in the first instance by my fellow Rotarian Fred Ainslie of Scotsec and his manageress Diana Provest. (It turned out that she had been in St Cuthbert's Girl Guides, and I had christened her husband in Cramond). Of the greatest practical assistance throughout has been my grand-daughter, Jane Young, during her enforced absence from her Business Administration course in Aberdeen, owing to that debilitating disease called ME. Once the full manuscript was available I am greatly indebted to Mr R D Kernahan O.B.E., formerly editor of 'Life and Work', for the benefit of his experienced advice. I am specially grateful to my old Colleague and fellow ex-Moderator, the Very Rev. David Steel, D.D., Ll.D., for so graciously writing the Foreword. If this book brings any interest or amusement to its readers, the credit is largely due to these kind friends.

Chapter 1

It's all in the Genes

On 12 May 1905, my father, the Rev. Robert Small, was working in his study, in the Abbey Manse, North Berwick, on a lecture he was preparing on John Knox. The nurse put her head round the door and announced: 'John Knox has arrived.' Some forty years later, when I went for the first time to preach in the lovely old Chapel of St. Andrews University, just as I moved out of my stall, the Principal, Donald Baillie, whispered: 'Don't forget, you are going into John Knox's pulpit.' Years later still, I stood in the quadrangle of the Assembly Hall, under the very shadow of the statue of Knox, and shook hands with the Pope.

Looking back now, having lived from the first decade to the last of the most momentous century in human history, I feel a sense of history, of not coming into the world to exist in a vacuum, of possessing roots, of belonging. At the same time I am aware, all through, of living in a changing world, of having a responsibility to all who came before, to those with whom I have shared these years of change, and a challenge from those who shall come after. None of these feelings have been often conscious, but appear, looking back, like the wake seen from the stern of a ship, or the pattern emerging in a woman's knitting.

Tracing this back, beginning with my father studying Knox, I realise that history was already in the family; it had got itself into the genes. Grandfather Small was the son of a weaver in Portmoak, near Kinross. He put himself through St. Andrews University, then went back on the staff as a lecturer in mathematics. He told my father that quite often he would be working late into the night, wrestling with some difficult problem of mathematics. Eventually he would give up in despair and go to bed. He found himself wakening in the morning with the problem solved – his mind had gone on working like a computer while he was asleep. I seem to have inherited that particular gene, because I have known the same thing happen,

1

whether it was the problem of fixing firmly a patch in an awkward position on the bottom of our boat in Iona, or mending a strained relationship between two of my members.

He changed his life-style and studied for the Ministry at the Synod Hall, on the site of the famous 'Hole in the Ground' (now filled in) in Castle Terrace. His first charge was in Southend in the Mull of Kintyre, where he raised a family of four sons and two daughters on an annual stipend of £120. He managed to save even from this small sum, and put his savings in the City of Glasgow Bank, which failed, so that thousands of little people like him lost all that they had saved. He moved to Edinburgh, first to a church in Portsburgh, then to Gilmore Place (now the Free Presbyterian Church). He then undertook a very demanding assignment – he extracted meticulously from the dusty archives of Synods, Presbyteries, Kirk Sessions, and Boards of Management of all the congregations of the Secession and Relief Churches, which became the United Presbyterian Church, the entire history of that whole church – the only such history in existence. For this *magnum opus* his Alma Mater awarded him a DD.

In later life he and his family became founder members of Greenbank Church in Edinburgh, where I have been a member since retirement. He died when I was fourteen days old, and left me an interesting legacy. The name of the baby was a matter of heated argument between my parents. It was still the accepted tradition that the first born son was named exactly after his father, grandfather, and so on, but mother was resisting. My father came back from Grandpa's funeral and said blithely: 'Well, Minnie dear, there were seven plain Robert Smalls at the funeral, including the corpse.' 'That settles it,' replied my mother, 'this child is going to have another name.' There was a family, well-to-do and very friendly, who came to North Berwick every summer from Accrington. They sent wonderful hampers of goodies to the parents at Christmas and splendid toys to us children, so they were special. The name of the son was 'Leonard' and that's where I got the name. One final word concerning my paternal grandfather. He was obviously a talented mathematical scholar, and quite certainly a very able historian, but he had two defects – he did not have a note of music, or an ounce of humour!

My father followed him into the Ministry, educated at James Gillespie's High School for Boys, then at George Watson's College, where he was one of the first pupils when it became a Day School, situated in Archibald Place, where the famous rivalry with Heriot's began. In 1991 I gave the Watson's Founder's Day Oration! He did an MA degree at Edinburgh University, winning the prize for poetry . . . a gift inherited by his youngest great-grandson, Christopher. After doing a student assistantship in Palmerston Place Church, he went to his first charge in Ecclefechan, where Thomas Carlyle and his father had been members. In 1895 he moved to a most unusual situation in Bonnington UP Church, Leith (a Church which, like sadly many, no longer exists). He went to be colleague and successor to Dr Hutchinson, who had married lashings of money – so much so that he and his wife owned a steam yacht, built at Ramage and Ferguson's and named *Hersilia* but known to everyone in Leith as 'Her siller'. They went cruising in the Norwegian fjords. In the evenings they played whist, and one evening they had dealt a hand and turned up one card to decide trump but no more, when the gong rang for dinner. During the meal my father slipped out on some excuse, went into the saloon, and dealt everyone a full suit. When they came back through he watched their faces as each gathered up the cards, especially the player with thirteen trumps. Now, he certainly didn't get that inventive mischief from his dour father but he has passed it on to at least one of his grandsons! While in Leith he contracted a very grave peritonitis, so critical they could not take him to hospital but operated, literally, on the kitchen table. For weeks he was at death's door till his GP, Dr Stewart said: 'I don't think you are going to die immediately – I give you six months.' He moved to North Berwick and outlived Dr Stewart by 55 years! He took with him to North Berwick a wife and his first child, Winifred, so it is time to introduce the second set of genes.

My mother was one of a family of thirteen, but that was a bit of a cheat, for there were two mothers with seven in the first family, six in the second. Her father, James McEwen, was the son of a joiner in Kirkcudbright, who became Provost. I still have some of his tools, with his name stamped on the handle. He must have passed on his skills generously, for I myself and all my family, are widely proficient at all forms of DIY. He was born in 1830, and at the age of fifteen walked from Kirkcudbright to Glasgow to go to University, sending his trunk by the carrier, which cost him 6*d*. He kept a notebook of all his expenses which I still have, so I know what he spent his money on between 1845 and 1848. His digs, all in, cost 5*s*. 10½*d*. When he moved to Edinburgh to the Synod Hall, he had to pay for his style, for they went up to 6*s*. 0½*d*. The academic year finished at Easter – you spent the summer working to keep yourself in meal (and herring if better off) during the next Session. He was ordained at twenty-one and lived to be ninety-three, so he was ordained for the phenomenal period of seventy-two years.

His first charge was at Pathhead, Ford, Midlothian; from there he moved to East Bank, Hawick. It was there that his first wife died, leaving him with seven children. He then married Margaret Melrose, the daughter of a well known engineering firm; her brother went on to be Provost Melrose of Hawick, which I always thought rather odd. For many years Grandpa was famous as 'the preacher who preached the washing back on the line'. Someone reported to him that someone had stolen a poor widow's washing . . . on Sunday he was fairly 'dingin' the blads' about the decline of modern morals and the depths of iniquity to which this unknown miscreant had sunk. On Monday morning the washing was back on the line . . . effective preaching with a vengeance! From Hawick he moved to Sydney Place, Dennistoun, Glasgow. He retired at ninety, having decided he had done enough. He lived on till I was a student, and I had the privilege of knowing this grand old man. I once asked him how he had managed to go on for seventy-two years turning out the reams of addresses he must have produced, remembering how mother described him walking the study floor of a Saturday night, doing what was known as 'mandating', committing to memory a thirty-minute sermon, which then poured out of him from the pulpit. With a twinkle in his eye he reassured this trembling beginner: 'Laddie – I had an inexhaustible subject.'

Mother was one of a family of four girls and two boys; the girls were all very good-looking. Their mother used to live in a kind of spin-off of fame. One member of the first family, Sir John B. McEwen, was for many years the Principal of the Royal College of Music in London, and a composer of some note. Granny used to refer with a proprietary air to 'my son, Sir John' – though he was not her son at all. She was a typical Victorian, prim, proper, habitually disapproving. When a small child she was chided for some misdemeanour and sent up to bed. She sat in her nightie at the open window and hoped she would catch pneumonia and die and they would all be sorry. It didn't work, she lived to be eighty-nine and kept us all in order. She was staying with us one time when the parents were away and we were being looked after by a grand old Scotswoman, Miss Shields, who was a wonderful cook. One day she laid on the table an ashet bearing something with a bowl on top which, being lifted, revealed an apple dumpling, like the haggis, 'warm, reekin', rich'. We children all exclaimed: 'O we do love apple dumpling.' Down went the corners of Granny's mouth: 'Children – keep love for higher things.' I have been accused of having a Puritanical streak because of my inability to accept some modern practices just because 'Everybody does it.' Clearly – blame Granny.

Mother, somehow, finished her education in Germany, and always read her German Bible in the pew. She was a good mezzo-soprano; she trained and taught as a domestic science teacher, and wisely passed on her expertise to all four of her children; we boys were taught to cook, bake, wash, iron, darn and mend. I have good cause to bless her now that I look after myself. So there you have the varied background of my life . . . weaving, solving problems, using tools, making music, searching records, baking shortbread, preaching the Word . . . it's all there in the genes . . . a musical composer and a dry historian with not a note of music . . . how do these genes get on?

Chapter 2

Formative Years

North Berwick in the first twenty years of this century was a good place in which to be born and grow up. It was a community of about 2,000, centring round the harbour, with a hinterland of the fertile acres of East Lothian. It was a bracing, healthy place, though cold in the winter on the edge of the wild North Sea. It was small enough for people to know each other, yet not so small as to become ingrown. Its community life got an annual shot in the arm through the influx of summer visitors . . . note, I did not say 'tourists'. That would demean the ethos of this fashionable resort in the years before World War I. People like the McAlpines, already mentioned, Coats of Paisley, Weirs of Glasgow, Forrester Patons of Alloa, would take a house for two or three months, bring their staff, and enrich local life, not just in money terms.

Let me illustrate what I am trying to express, for it is part of a lost world. Many of these distinguished visitors came each year to the Abbey Church, and always paid a courtesy call at the Manse. By clever family planning on my part, my pram was always standing outside the front door throughout the summer, and these kindly folk would never pass without putting a coin for luck in the baby's pudgy palm . . . no small change, but either a sovereign or a half-sovereign . . . highly dangerous, for the child might have swallowed it. Careful watch was kept; the moment the gate shut the coin was retrieved and disposed of . . . all this without my knowledge or consent. Nineteen years later, on going to University, I was presented with a Savings Bank Account Book, with a sum far beyond the reach of a normal student. With it I was able to take out an insurance policy, and maintain the premiums till my stipend took them over. The year the policy matured the house in Iona which we had occupied as summer tenants came on the market and this rare capital sum enabled us to make an offer and secure our most precious possession . . . all dating back to the pram at the Manse door in 'the good old days'.

One stage further on in my hobnobbing with gentry a lady, Mrs Crawford, who later gifted The Elms to the Kirk for an Eventide Home, and who was spending three summer months in a big house near the Marine Hotel, kindly invited the Manse boys to call and visit her. I would be about ten and Colin seven. We were well drilled in what to do and what not to do, and because the Manse never had a telephone Mother said: 'You can stay to tea if Mrs Crawford asks you.' So off we went to be received at the door by a butler in full canonicals. Colin, not unnaturally assuming he was the proprietor, shook hands, whereupon Jeeves nearly took a fit from laughing, but managed to usher us into the palatial drawing-room, where we waded across ankle-deep carpet and I greeted our gracious hostess with: 'How do you do, Mrs Crawford. Mummy says we can stay to tea if you ask us.' There was a choking withdrawal of Jeeves, to return later with a tea trolley bearing triangular sandwiches like Cape triangular stamps, accompanied by tiny afternoon tea serviettes, embroidered with C, obviously for Crawford. We got away with no more gaffes, went home and proceeded to 'clype' on each other. I expressed my horror at Colin shaking hands with the butler, and he at my opening gambit with our hostess. Then Colin rounded it off very happily by taking from his pocket a serviette and saying: 'Well, anyway, it was very kind of them giving us these wee hankies with our initial on them.'

Was I training then for moving in still Higher Society? No. I did not say to the Queen in the drawing-room at Balmoral: 'How do you do, Your Majesty. My wife says I can stay the weekend if you ask me.' One more memory of that bygone era. The Forrester-Paton brothers of Paton and Baldwin fame came, Alexander in July with a lovely old Rolls Royce and a chauffeur in grey uniform called Izatt, John in August with a big Armstrong Siddeley, with a green-uniformed chauffeur called Morrison. Next year they changed months. They never failed to give my father and his family the use of the car and chauffeur for a whole day. These were the highlights of our childhood . . . we usually went for a picnic in the Lammermuirs, father sitting in front beside the driver, returning the salutes of the AA patrolmen 'as to the manner born' on £250 a year.

There were many other regulars, famous people whom we used to watch from the Manse windows driving off from the first tee, later to appear in the pages of the *Tatler* or the *Bystander* though it never showed you where the ball went. For the locals, too, life had all sorts of perks. A season ticket for the Burgh Golf Course was 5*s.*; the swimming pool was 7*s.* 6*d.*; tennis was dear at 15*s.* The visitors brought a higher standard of play, and added generally to the quality of living.

North Berwick, seeming from the map to be on a kind of bypass, might well have been thought remote from world events . . . not so. I remember standing in the Manse garden in the moonlight watching the Zeppelin making its landfall before going on to bomb Edinburgh; watching through the binoculars the British Fleet limping back from Jutland, the *Tiger* towed stern-first for her bows were blown away; studying a full-page spread in the local paper with passport-size photos of men from the County killed in the battle of the Somme. But the whole of that War and all since for me is symbolised and encapsulated in its mixture of wicked waste and heroic sacrifice in the end of July 1914 which brought me an experience I can never forget. Home on leave were two men from the Forces . . . Johnnie Bell in all the scarlet and gold of the dress-uniform of the Royal Scots Greys, and Norman Arundel in the familiar uniform of the Royal Navy, a wireless telegraphist on the cruiser *Amphion*. They came to supper at the Manse before returning to their posts. I can still see them in the front hall of the Manse, teaching us two boys to do their different salutes . . . the soldier salutes palm-out, the sailor palm-down as if shading his eyes to look over the sea. On 8 August, the War just four days old, my father came to me and said: 'You'll never see Norman Arundel again. His ship has been blown up and every man is lost.' Then he added what I thought was strange to say to a boy of nine: 'The one thing I want you to remember about that man is that he died for you.'

I believe it to be deep mysterious reality, I cannot forget it, and I think of it in the Silence every Remembrance Day.

Nor was one immune from the trials and tribulations of ordinary living. My younger sister, Nancy, much the smaller of very non-identical twins with Colin, was never strong and had what was then called 'infantile paralysis'. One of my earliest, haunting memories is of my father plunging this scrap of humanity, torn by convulsion fits, into hot and cold water alternately, all that could be done, and seeing the agony on his face. She was never fully fit, and when she was twenty-six he went in to waken her and found her dead, curled up on the floor beside her pet fox terrier. There were other less traumatic issues of which one could not help being aware, like the lasting distinctions between the denominations. My father was in the Abbey Church, the old United Presbyterian Church; Nevile Davidson's father was in the Blackadder, the old Free . . . these two belonged till 1929 to the United Free Church, but had no great comings and goings. The Rev. James R. Burt was in the old Parish Church, now St. Andrew's. In all my boyhood I was only twice in the Parish Church . . . forgivable because it was a Scout Parade Service. During the War my father was on the minimum stipend of

£250; James Burt with the tiend stipend and the inflated price of grain was on £1200 . . . talk about differentials. The mere idea of daring to enter St. Baldred's Episcopal Church, where all the 'posh' people went, would never enter anyone's head. The Roman Catholic Chapel of our Lady Star of the Sea was almost opposite the School gates, and you hurried past, lest the priest saw you and 'put the evil eye on you'. That was the kind of atmosphere in a small community in 'the good old days'. I am thankful to have lived to take a Service as Moderator in my father's church with everyone there, both clerical and lay.

There were many interests beginning then and there which were to last. One still with me is Scouting. I joined the 1st North Berwick Troop in 1917. It had been founded in August 1908, one of the earliest in the country. I enjoyed it and took it seriously, so that I was able, as a King's Scout, to be one of the 250 Scouts from Scotland who attended the First World Jamboree at Olympia, with the Scottish camp in the old Deer Park at Richmond. It was a tremendous thrill, to be one of 8,000 boys from all over the world, especially the morning the Chief Scout, B.P. himself, came to inspect the Scottish camp, and the forty-one of us King's Scouts formed a Guard of Honour at the entrance. B.P. got down off his horse and walked along the line, shaking hands with each of us, and asking about our Troop. At fifteen I wanted to keep a glove for ever on that left hand he had shaken. I went on to be Troop Leader, Assistant Scoutmaster, and Scoutmaster, and led the Troop from East Lothian at the 21st Birthday Jamboree at Arrowe Park, Birkenhead. I had to sever my connection with North Berwick Scouts when I went to live in Edinburgh, but I started a Troop from scratch in St. John's, Bathgate, and acted also as District Commissioner for SW West Lothian. In Kilmarnock there was a strong BB bias, but I kept my hand in as DC for NW Ayrshire. Then when we went to Cramond I started a Troop with eleven boys in the local Primary School. When we left it had grown so much it was divided into three. St. Cuthbert's Troop was in the last dying stages because of depopulation, so I switched to being a kind of permanent conductor of large Parades, with a central Church which could hold 2,500 Scouts and Cub Scouts. I learned early on the near impossibility of one person receiving on one almsdish the cumulative weight of bags holding 2,500 old pennies, or their decimal equivalent. I am now a Vice-President of the Edinburgh City Scout Council, and President of Haymarket District. Last year I was awarded the Silver Wolf for long and distinguished service to Scouting . . . a far cry from No. 8 in the Owl patrol who cleaned the porridge dixie . . .

Another great kindred interest was sport, at which I was a late starter

Outside St. George's Chapel, Windsor, after receiving Scout supreme award, Silver Wolf

because of illness in earlier childhood. I turned up for a School practice, and when the sports master asked what position I played I had to confess I had never played before. 'Well,' he said, 'you're tall enough, you can go in goal.' But for that casual advice this book would never have had this odd title. Playing became almost an addiction, till in my last year at school I was playing for the School in the morning, and for the town team, the Bass Rock, in the afternoon. In the summer tennis was all the go. We were lucky to have good courts and plenty of good players among the visitors who raised the standards considerably. There were, for example, the Weir sisters from Newlands, Jeanette, Gina and Marie, who were representative standard. My own partner, in the North Berwick team and in many tournaments, was Jean Bertram, who was later to become Deputy Head of George Watson's Ladies College. She had a wicked spin service (underhand) which spun away from the receiver and let me practise my goalkeeping techniques and cut the return off at the net.

Last, but by no means least, there was the sea and the boats. From an early age I crewed for Mr John Whitecross, who sailed a 26-foot yacht called the *Water Kelpie*. Mucking about in boats is an excellent training for

North Berwick High School Soccer Team (RLS Captain)

the business of living; you learn the hard way what you can and cannot do in a smallish boat, not in a sheltered lake, but in open water, like the mouth of the North Sea or the fringes of the great Atlantic as around Iona. You have to know where the rocks are at all stages of the tide, to reckon with the force of winds and currents, to deal with sudden emergencies. My family all laughed at me for being so fussy. To my great delight, they have been just as punctilious with their own children. I used to be dropped off at the pierhead to go round and bring the dinghy to the moorings . . . I never thought I would graduate to sailing round the world, far less conning a submarine at 50 fathoms.

Because the sea played so large a part in my early life, perhaps I may be forgiven for telling of two experiences with the sea, one as a spectator, the other as a participant. In the days before boat engines, when a fishing boat was propelled by one huge tan sail, two such boats from Cockenzie were fishing near the May Island when a fierce north-east gale sprang up suddenly and drove them relentlessly, amid huge seas, towards the Platcock

Rocks at the approach to North Berwick harbour. One was called the *Pansy*, the other the *Trust-on*. The *Pansy* cleared the point and was dashed with such force against the remains of Galloway's pier that the men were able to jump ashore and scramble to safety. The *Trust-on* was dashed on a rock right at the Point and impaled on it, too far out to be reached from the rocks or for the men on board to risk jumping into the sea, with the waves breaking over everything. They were saved by a bit of quick thinking by the chief coastguard who got a length of strong but not too heavy rope, fastened one end to a ringbolt in the rock, and flung the rest over the boat, shouting what he wanted done. One man clambered up the tall mast, passed the end through the block, pulled all the slack through and flung it back to the rock, where the rescuers laid on the end, and, using the 'through and back' purchase, every time a big wave lifted the boat off the impaling rock, pulled the great mast over, stage by stage, till it formed a bridge over which the men from the wreck crawled to safety. All of this we watched from the Manse windows. When I visited Cockenzie as Moderator I wanted to express how Christ, coming down to earth, getting below our burdens and going back to God, had, using the same 'through and back' pattern, given God a new purchase on human life, so I told that story. At the end of the meeting an old man came to me with tears running down his face and said: 'I was the skipper of one of those boats, and you had every detail right except that you mixed up the names of the boats.' We worked it out that I must have been six and a half at the time.

The other unforgettable bout with the sea came nearly ten years later. We were wakened by the sound of rockets on a wild Christmas morning, to find that another of those terrible north-east gales had driven a Norwegian cargo ship onto the rocks just opposite the island of Fidra. The Scouts acted as auxiliaries to the rocket crew so we were soon on the go, getting the lorry with all the gear along to the site and down the bents as near the beach as we could get. Then it was a matter of carrying everything down to the point of the rocks. The ship, high out of the water because she was 'in ballast', i.e. with no cargo, was hard and fast on the outer reef, with a great stretch of surf between her and safety, with great seas breaking over her. Going as far out as possible the chief coastguard (the same as saved the fishermen from their wreck) set up his tripod with its rocket, and set it streaming straight towards the wreck. The wind caught it and blew it uselessly past the bows like a paper streamer.

There was one box of light line left, one other chance of making saving contact. The coastguard set up his second rocket, aimed it into the wind past the stern, paused several times with his slow-match ready, waiting for the slightest lull, and lit the rocket which seemed to be missing completely.

Then the wind swept it right across midships, where the crew caught it, pulled in the light line, then a heavier, and then the great hawser, with a board, lettered in the languages of the main seafaring nations, telling them to make it fast round the mast and make sure that the flanged pulley that was to carry the breeches-buoy on it was running free. There was a long stretch of rope to the shore with a deep sag which it was our job to tighten. An anchor with only one fluke was firmly fixed in a crevice in the rocks and to it was fixed a great block with the rope running through it some three times – the same 'through and back' principle; we all hauled on the rope till the great hawser, the bridge to safety, rose out of the sea, and the crew, one at a time, began to cross in the breeches-buoy. Half were over when the buoy broke and the man fell into the surf. Happily he was swept back against the ship, to be hauled on board and have another chance. From that point on one of the men on the rocks tied a life-line to his waist and waded out into the sea, armpit high, to help each man to safety. The captain came last, carrying the ship's collie in his arms. I have often looked back on that experience as a kind of acted parable of the way God saves us. He begins with something weak and frail – the thread of a tiny child's life; His grip, His contact grows stronger stage by stage till He offers us 'amazing grace'. Through the Bible in all the languages of the world He tells us what we have to do to lay hold of it; when we fall He risks His life to bring us safe ashore. All this near obsession with the sea brings me to the most important choice I had to make. It happened in the setting of school.

North Berwick High School was a typical good country school, with some three hundred pupils, offering a good, sound, all-round education, for which my father paid 30 shillings a quarter, so I must confess to the unforgivable sin of going to a fee-paying school. One teacher I remember was Marie O. Campbell, who taught us English. We all disliked her, she was so sarcastic, but she made me love English, which has been a lifelong blessing. The Rector, Thomas S. Glover, was away on Service for the latter part of the War, and his place was taken by . . . my father.

I had always meant to go into the Navy, but there were problems. I spent a great deal of my childhood running through a list of illnesses . . . bronchitis, asthma, pleurisy, paratyphoid. I was put to bed for six months with what was then called 'growing pains', but which I was later told would have been rheumatic fever. The time for entry to Dartmouth Naval College was $12\frac{1}{2}-13\frac{1}{2}$ which for me fell in 1917, and anyway I was not fit enough. So the Navy was out and I had no alternative. It was at this stage in your school career when your future course is fitted to your plans for a job, and I was under pressure.

At the beginning of the Session we had a new Latin master (my fifth) and after his first class he stopped me, saying: 'Are you the boy who wants to learn Greek?' I was so surprised I reacted almost rudely: 'What . . . me, sir? Oh no, not me, sir.' Then I recovered and started to think . . . why would I want to learn Greek? If I was going to teach Classics – a fate worse than death. Otherwise, only if I was going to be a minister. The idea niggled away. I started watching my father and what he did more closely. I listened to him preaching; he was always interesting and could be very dramatic. He was once describing how David picked his stone, fitted it into his sling and, taking careful aim at the bully Goliath, whirled the sling and let fly, all dramatically mimed. At the release of the stone a whole row of people in the gallery ducked their heads! I thought: 'This preaching is a fascinating thing to do.' My father took me on some of his visits to old folk, and I was hooked. I went back to the Latin teacher, and he started to teach me Greek. I sat at his table while he gave a Latin class an exercise, then spared me a few moments . . . not an ideal way to learn.

It turned out that the only previous Greek scholar had been Nevile Davidson and this small country school went on to pride itself that in that period of its history it had two Greek scholars, both of whom went on to be Moderator of the General Assembly, a Chaplain to the Queen, and the minister of a large and historic Church, Nevile in Glasgow Cathedral, myself in St. Cuthbert's. I want to make it plain that there was no 'clear call for me', no dramatic decision, no red-letter day, only the quiet, slow, steady growth of an idea that would not go away, and could not be resisted. I wanted to be like my father, to do what he did, and find it as enjoyable and rewarding as he clearly did. This was what I had come to want to do, and had to do.

Chapter 3

Training to realise this clear purpose

The transition from school to University, as often, was not easy. At school your work is still largely 'dished out' to you – at University you have to arrange your own programme of study. My situation was further complicated by the fact that during that first year I travelled daily by train: not a good idea, and an appalling waste of time. As a result, I did not start some of the set books until too late and failed First Ordinary Latin, which I had to repeat the next year (I won the Class Medal, but that was a bit of a cheat). Of all my professors I remember with great affection Sandy Mair in Greek, a truly wonderful teacher.

One of the highlights of the final year was going with a group of students under Professor Richmond for five weeks over Easter to Rome and Naples. That provided another illustration of the contrast of resources for students between then and now. Someone had left a fund whose interest accrued every fourth year enough to send four students from each of the four years on this special assignment. This was very generous, but you had to supplement the grant by £10 from your own resources. I didn't have £10. I had a bursary of £18 per annum from Lothian Road Church, long since exhausted. I referred to my father who said: 'Say you're going but I don't know where I am going to get the £10.' (This was one twenty-fifth of his annual income.) Came the first week of March, when you had to put down your money and stop talking. On the Monday my father still hadn't the £10. On Tuesday an old lady who lived in Dirleton Avenue died and, as there was no other Minister available, my father took the funeral. In the horse-driven cab coming back from the cemetery the lawyer handed my father an envelope, saying: 'By the terms of the old lady's will that is to go to the Minister who takes her funeral.' And that's how I got the money to go to Rome . . . changed days indeed.

After that wasteful and frustrating first year I moved into digs at 10

Gladstone Terrace, on the south side of the Meadows, not far from the Sick Children's Hospital. My landlady was a Miss Thomson who took me on at the same rates as my sister – thirty shillings a week for breakfast and high tea on weekdays, all meals on Sunday. I was therefore able to settle in and take a fuller part in the life of the University. One of the main interests, naturally, for the not-yet-holy goalie, was football. Not having played in the Freshers' Trial through staying at home, I played my first game for the 3rd XI. I then had the cheek to write to the Secretary and say: 'I was accustomed to a better brand of football.' I was called to a Wednesday practice, went straight into the 1st XI and never came out, going on to win three 'Blues' and to captain the Section. I had great fun, with ordinary matches, inter-Varsity Field Days, and Meal Monday Tours to Durham, Leeds and Manchester and formed many lasting friendships. When I was Moderator we held a reunion dinner for all who had played between 1925 and 1935. There was a grand response, and it was great meeting again after forty years and seeing how life had turned out for each. A few years later there were similar celebrations when Jim Matheson, another player from those vintage years, was Moderator.

When Stanley Baldwin was installed as Rector in the McEwan Hall I was put in front of one lectern, with Callum McQueen, the shinty goalkeeper, in front of the other to field as much as possible of the random missiles: bags of flour, soot, peasemeal, along with a few cod-heads, even a live cockerel from the top gallery. There were outrageous students in those days too. During another Rectorial Election Tom Campbell, President of the Liberal Association, was abducted from his digs in his pyjamas and taken out to a lonely cottage on the Lang Whang road, and kept there till it was all over. He went on to be minister of Fenwick and played with me in the Kilmarnock tennis team. He was later for many years in Dundee, and was widely known as the writer of a regular column in the *People's Friend*. I came out of University with an MA degree, with 1st Class Honours in Classics, and a greatly widened experience of human life, for a son of the Manse from a 'hick town' like North Berwick.

On going to New College I moved into the New College Settlement in the Pleasance, then one of the worst slums in Europe. Just across from us was a great, gaunt tenement block with forty 'homes' and only one toilet. Prestonfield, the first slum clearance scheme, was just being built, and the families were beginning to move out. We ran a concert for the children on a Saturday evening . . . I can see and smell those children yet, with a man's jacket, the sleeves cut short, for an overcoat. They kept on coming back from their fine new homes. When we asked: 'Why do you keep coming back from the room and air you have out there?', they replied: 'It's o'or quate oot there. There's nae fechts nor funerals oot there' . . . a fight or a funeral alone brought drama to the slum. I was made aware of a side of city life which, all the way from the Pleasance, through Savannah, Georgia, to Dum Dum, Calcutta, has never failed to make me feel shocked and shamed and somehow guilty.

There were sixteen students in our year, and we were a rare lot, for we were the last students of the old United Free Church in New College; we were the first licensed into the reunited Church of Scotland, we acted as stewards at the Union Assembly, and I eventually became the first Moderator out of that generation. In the summer of our final year Alex Coutie, Denzil Patrick, George Sloan and myself were sent to an International Theological Course in the University of Berlin, where we heard 'greats' like Deismann, von Harnack, von Seeberg, and Lietzmann, on instantaneous translation. We realised the 'vacuum' of depression and lack of purpose in which our German fellow-students were living; that was 1929, and we never heard the name of Adolf Hitler; by 1933 he had filled this emptiness and was Chancellor of all Germany. At home we had Hugh Mackintosh, Adam Welch, Hugh Watt, Willie Manson, Danny Lamont, Harry Miller, and Principal Alex Martin. Near the end of our course he asked us each to write an essay on 'My call to the Ministry'. By this time my sensitivity over my lack of any dramatic experience, over against my fellow-students, was so great that I wrote frankly about this. The old man sent for me and said: 'You are making a common mistake in imagining that the only way into the Christian life and the Ministry is by a sudden, dramatic experience, like Paul on the Damascus road, whereas with your background the natural thing would be to grow into it gradually, as you clearly have done.' I put this on record to help anyone who may feel as I then did.

One of the highlights of that final year was an Easter Retreat in Iona. Sir David Russell, of the papermaking firm in Markinch, had made funds available to enable four students from each of the final years in the Divinity Colleges to spend a week in Iona with two professors; we had W.M. McGregor and Hugh Watt, an interesting combination. For me that was the beginning of a life-long addiction. We travelled through Mull in T model Fords, and it took us four and a half hours from Craignure to Fionnphort . . . with luck you do it now in one hour. We stayed in the Columba Hotel, played a golf match against the Islanders, and gave a concert for them in the Village Hall, recently opened. I played the part of the hero in a stupendous melodrama, *The Vengeance of Jasper McBrayne*.

The heroine was George Fraser, son of that great missionary, Donald Fraser; George, sadly, died young. Two of the students from Aberdeen 'had the Gaelic'. They cut up an old sheep's fleece to make white beards and hair, donned old sailors' caps and did a scurrilous running commentary on all the rest of us in Gaelic, to the hilarious delight of the locals. That must have been the first get-together of students from both sides of the now reunited Church of Scotland.

As a student in my final years at New College I was naturally a keen observer of the debates in the United Free Assembly leading up to the actual Union, debates that often became heated, so strong were the feelings on either side. I had to endure the hurt and anger at hearing my own father being shouted down – he expressed himself so strongly about endangering the voluntary principle and accepting involvement with the State. I was to realise later what sacrifices could be made out of loyalty to these principles. When we went to Cramond I learned that my predecessor in 1843, George Muirhead, came out, leaving himself with neither Church nor Manse, no stipend nor pension. He signed the Act of Demission first after the Assembly officials for, at eighty-three, he was the oldest minister who came out at the Disruption. They at least let him come back to be buried in his own Kirkyard. On his headstone is carved his motivation: 'Being fully persuaded in his own mind.' My father eventually decided there was more to be gained by going in than by staying out, and remained a loyal servant of the Church of Scotland to the end of his sixty-nine years of Ordination. A few years before he died at ninety-three, there was only one minister longer ordained. He used to say: 'I keep looking at the back page of the *Scotsman* hopefully, but that old chap in Perth is hanging on too long. However,' he added blithely, 'while there's death, there's hope.' The old chap in Perth obligingly died in good time, and for his last eighteen months the minister who, in May 1905, had been writing a lecture on John Knox, was the father of the Kirk.

Chapter 4

Red Letter Days

On 1 March 1929, three events took place which marked that as a red letter day in my life – they are not listed in order of importance, the title of this book notwithstanding.

I received a printed postcard from the Secretary of the Scottish Football Association, who at that time selected the amateur as well as the professional international teams. It informed me that I had been chosen to play for Scotland v England at Elland Road, Leeds. This obviously requires to be placed in its setting. At University we played in the East of Scotland League, where one of the regular referees, Bob Innes, had often seen me play. He had become secretary of St. Bernard's Football Club and, as I was leaving University to go to New College, he persuaded me to sign and play as an amateur in what was a professional team. This was a very old Club, about to celebrate its 60th anniversary, currently playing in the upper half of the Second Division of the Scottish League. Their ground was The Gymnasium in Fettes Row, and they enjoyed a sizeable and loyal following of about 3,000, mainly in the Stockbridge area.

It was an interesting and valuable experience, broadening my knowledge of the man in the street (or on the terracing behind the goals). My fellow-players were many of them miners, several from Newtongrange Star, and they must have found a divinity student a real cuckoo in the nest, but they treated me with friendliness, and obviously respected what I stood for. As happened with Eric Liddell in the dressing-rooms of the toughest athletic clubs, what was normal language was carefully moderated, and the same attitude generally prevailed among the spectators. Once, when playing against Raith Rovers at Stark's Park, Kirkcaldy, there was a mix-up in the goalmouth and the ball went past, no one sure whether it was a goal kick or a corner kick. Voice from behind the goal: 'Hey, referee . . . ask the goalie. He's a meenister . . . he'll no' tell ye a lee.' Having played for the Club on grounds all over the country from August 1928 I was selected to play at Leeds as indicated, and duly played. There was in those days a huge crowd, and I was so nervous I could hardly stand; we got beaten 3-1. Looking back I wonder about this reaction. Since then I have been in much more daunting situations, and generally faced them with surprising calmness. Perhaps I share the ambivalent attitude of Mary Slessor who couldn't venture across Sauchiehall Street but stood firm between two warring tribes, refusing to let them at each others' throats . . . when she was on the Lord's business, He would see her through. Unfortunately I have no record of this extra special (one off) occasion, because my Gold Medal was stolen when I was away in Australia. I have nothing but the Lion Rampant Badge from my jersey – the moths got the jersey long ago.

The second special event on that momentous date was that I received my first appointment in the Ministry. I was appointed Student Assistant in St. Catherine's in Grange Church. My 'bishop' was the Rev. Dr William Ewing. His courage was not in question, for he had won a Military Cross when serving with Allenby in the Holy Land; he was, at the same time, very emotional. Reading any moving passage of Scripture caused him to weep copiously. On one occasion he was reading David's lament for Absalom and broke down completely so that he could not go on. I had to come up from the choir and take over from him. This was early good experience of coping with sudden emergencies. My main duties centred on a mission in the Causewayside where, among other activities, I had to run a Children's Church. The range of ages was from three to thirteen, and to keep their attention was an almost impossible task. I adopted an idea which my father regularly followed during the summer. For example, in a golfing centre like North Berwick, he took into the pulpit what would now be called a sandwedge, and used the text: 'Thou tookest me up out of the fearful pit.' A visual aid gave the younger ones something to look at, and the older ones something to learn.

I have followed this custom all my life; in Cramond with the Cargilfield Prep. schoolboys we did six months on 'things you need for a voyage' beginning at New Year with a chart and ending with an engine-room telegraph! I think the most unforgettable was the sword of King Robert the Bruce which I borrowed from the Earl of Elgin for a youth parade in the Queen's Jubilee year. There was also an organisation for men, which was widely in vogue at that time, called the Pleasant Sunday Afternoon. It was informal in dress and style, usually there was a small orchestra and/or a soloist, and large numbers of working men attended and enjoyed it. It was one helpful example of an alternative to normal formal worship.

The third, and most important, of the special occasions dated 1 March 1929, was that I became engaged to be married. This obviously requires to be placed in its setting. When I came to stay in digs in Edinburgh I started to attend Lothian Road Church – now Filmhouse. I did so because of the longstanding friendship between my father and the minister, the Very Rev. Dr R. J. Drummond. A side benefit was that as a student from Lothian Road Church I qualified for the March Bursary of £18 per annum – untold wealth. To begin with I sat meekly in the Manse pew beside Mrs Drummond, who was a replica of the stately Queen Mary. During the General Strike in 1926 I had to stay over weekends in town and allowed myself to be inveigled into joining the choir. When the male voices turned round after singing to face the pulpit they sat in the row of chairs nearest to the communion table. The females, sopranos on the right, sat in the row behind. The one immediately behind me occasionally and quite accidentally kicked me under the chair. To that extent I became aware of a good looking young lady, aware and no more. After the choir party I saw her home, most unromantically as the distance was less than half a mile and we were closely chaperoned by her sister Lily and her fiancé, George Finlayson.

This is where the 'holy goalie' syndrome comes into play again. As captain of the Soccer Section I was ex officio a member of the Athletic Club Committee. In December they decided to hold a dance in early January and I had to find a partner. I had never taken a girl to a dance in my life, and did not know any potential partners, apart from this very flimsy connection with the 'girl in the choir'. I knew her Christian name was Jean; I did not know her surname, or where she lived, for they had removed. I had no idea what age she was – when my mother asked me I said, 'Anything from seventeen to twenty-seven' – she was in fact nineteen. Anyhow, I asked her if she would come to the dance and rather reluctantly she agreed and came. That was the beginning of the end and we got engaged on the date above mentioned which happened to be her twenty-first birthday. She was born at ten minutes after midnight on 1 March in a leap year, and her mother said that if she had not stopped kicking for fifteen minutes she would have been born on the fatal 29 February! She complained intermittently for quite a while about being done out of a twenty-first present, to which I always replied: 'What better twenty-first birthday gift than an engagement ring?'

Jean was born in Aberdeen and the family moved to Edinburgh when she was eighteen months old. Her father was a foreman bookbinder in Stewart's in George Street; her mother was a gem of a caring person from north Aberdeenshire. Jean was always sensitive about having left Boroughmuir

School when she was fourteen, as the family circumstances demanded, and having followed Lily into a course of training in ladies' outfitting in Darling's, one of the famous family businesses in Princes Street. She felt self-conscious alongside other wives of ministers or moderators, many of whom had been honours graduates, but she was given a splendidly relevant training. A very wise buyer taught these girls to study and know every regular customer as a person, to remember her likes and dislikes and her personal taste, and to study to meet her needs. It really was a priceless training for all that was involved in being my wife and it never failed her. She associated happily and easily with all sorts of people from the 'Wivies' in the Mission to the Queen herself. She just went on being her bonnie, warmhearted, caring self. During my year as Moderator she started with typical thoughtfulness a tea party during the Assembly for the wives of ex-Moderators, and did not forget widows and sisters. This function still goes on. She had the right background as a Sunday School teacher, a member of that famous organisation, the Girls' Association and, as mentioned, the choir. That first of March led on into forty-eight years of sharing in an incredible variety of interesting experiences, phenomenally wide travel around the world, sailing around one way and flying the other. It was a life of unbelievable richness, fully shared with her husband and family unto the next generation.

The following March we were licensed in St. Giles', the first group since the Union. That summer I preached for July and August in St. John's Church, Bathgate, where the Rev. John Lindsay had been Minister for forty-four years. During the War years he had been padre to the 10th Royal Scots, who were stationed for some time in North Berwick. Already a good friend of my father he used his study regularly for peace and quiet, and had come to know me as schoolboy and, later, student. He wanted me to succeed him, and went about it very cleverly. He told no one of his intention to retire but went off for two months to Canada in 1930, putting me in his place 'on approval' but secretly. Then in October I went off to Zurich to do the necessary study for a thesis which had to be given under the terms of the Senior Cunningham Fellowship. I stayed with the Baumgartner family; the mother had been at school in Germany with Mrs Lindsay, and they all spoke good English – which they refused to do, so I had to learn German. In three weeks I was taking lectures in theological German. The professor under whom I had chosen to study was Emil Brunner, and I was fortunate enough to get to know him personally. He was translating lectures he was to give in Britain and America, so he asked me to help him with the translation. He had four young sons who kept his feet on the ground. One asked him: 'Dad, is God everywhere?' 'Yes, my son.' 'Everywhere in

Zurich?' 'Yes, my son.' 'In this house, and this room?' 'Yes, my son.' 'Is He in this cup?' Rather put off, Dad still said: 'Yes, my son.' Whipping his hands on top of the cup, the boy exclaimed triumphantly: 'Right . . . I've got Him.' I regard Brunner as the finest preacher I ever heard . . . I queued at 8.00 a.m. for the 9.30 Service, and stood for forty-five minutes.

I managed to live for the six months of the winter semester on £90, saving the other half of the Cunningham Fellowship £180 in order to get married. I came home in March 1931 to do two important things – to find a church and to plan to get married. Instead the church found me. The planning of Mr Lindsay for the vacancy in St. John's, Bathgate, worked perfectly. The Vacancy Committee met and agreed that after forty-four years of one ministry they could be doing with a young man. That young chap they had last summmer seemed very promising; why bother searching further? Let's just call him. So we knew we were going to our first home in Bathgate in September and could safely plan to get married. This we did on 22 June in Lothian Road Church. It took three ministers to make sure that it would stick – Dr Drummond, who was the minister to both Jean and myself; Mr Lindsay, whom I was to succeed; and, obviously, my father. Having been married in the church which had played so large a part in our happily developing associations we went off on our honeymoon to Iona. We stayed in the Columba Hotel, as I had done as a student.

On Sunday, of course, we went to church in the Abbey, and sat in two of the choir stalls. When the visiting minister entered the church I realised it was Nevile Davidson, my old schoolmate. The highlight of our three weeks (which cost us 3 guineas a week, all in, for the hotel), was a visit to Staffa. As we stood in Fingal's Cave, that wonderful natural cathedral, we agreed that it would be wonderful to come some day with a full balanced choir and sing 'Ye Gates lift up your heads on high'. Fifty years later when a party of us with German visitors from Munich were staying in the Abbey, we went to Staffa with a balanced choir of forty voices and sang 'Ye Gates . . .'. I have always cherished the memory of that communion, our first service together as husband and wife. In June 1979, just months before Jean's thirteen year struggle with Parkinson's disease ended, we went to Iona. On the last Sunday I managed to get her wheelchair up the steep little hill, by Maclean's Cross, went in the back way to the Abbey, where there were no steps, and sat in the same two stalls as forty-eight years before to the day. Neither of us could know how wonderful it was to be, for it turned out to be the last time we were in church together at communion. That, of course, is jumping very far ahead and our story must now return to going to our first charge.

Chapter 5

Bathgate and the Depression

I was ordained in St. John's Church, Bathgate, on 10 September 1931.

It was a Congregation of the old United Presbyterian Church, strong and active, and the best giving in the Presbytery. It had a membership of 450, including many professional people among whom were no fewer than forty-five school teachers and two headmasters . . . the fact that the Rev. John Lindsay had been for many years the Convener of the Education Committee of the County Council may have been a contributory factor, but one must not get cynical. Very early on I came up against two problems concerning the membership, one comparatively minor, the other disastrous. Several of the office-bearers had been officers in the 1/10th Royal Scots stationed at North Berwick during the War, and it cannot have been easy for David Sutherland, James Wright, the town clerk, R.A. Brown, the rector of the Academy and sundry others, to 'Give his proper place' to a beginner aged twenty-six, whom they had known as a school laddie. It had to be achieved, as indeed it was, with plenty of mutual patience, if one was to exercise any real leadership among the changes that had to be made after a ministry of forty-four years.

The other problem arose from the vulnerable area of the old United Presbyterian constitution with its artificial separation of the sacred from the secular, enshrined in the two boards of the Kirk Session and the Board of Management. At our Annual Congregational Meeting I opened the proceedings with prayer, then retired and waited all evening in the Vestry lest some matter of business should arise that could be construed as sacred. There was a dispute over the organist in the Organ Committee, composed of three from each Board. The organist's wife appealed to Caesar in the form of one of the senior elders, who undertook to sort the matter out. He called a meeting of the Kirk Session and, when they were assembled in the Hall, back to back with the Manse, came to call me, without previous warning, to take the chair. I was away at an Induction, so they proceeded to hold a meeting without a Moderator and passed a vote of censure on the Managers for exceeding their authority. Because of the ensuing dispute I had eighteen special Session Meetings during my first year as a minister. What was much more serious, it produced a family feud which ran through the Congregation and infected everything. That was why, after only four years, I felt it was better to leave and let someone who had not been involved take over.

Much more serious than any squabbles within the Kirk was the current state of affairs in the early 30s in an industrial town like Bathgate. There were the North British Steel Works, Wolfe's Shovel Works, Livingston's Hosiery, Riddochhill coal mine, and several shale mines. I visited them all, to see where and under what conditions my folk were working – if they were working. Some stark memories stand out from those now distant days – a girl sitting all day and every day feeding into a chute pieces of scrap metal left when the shovel heads had been cut out, punching holes in discs, so making washers for the twisted nails to fix corrugated iron . . . a dull, routine job if ever there was one; miners working in a 'wet' pit, walking home off the night shift with their clothes frozen on them, then sitting cross-legged in a wooden tub in the middle of the kitchen floor, with the rafters festooned with clothes drying; men working with pneumatic guns, chipping the rough metal off the castings, their hands going on shaking long after they had finished; one of my elders, his hands protected with leather mittens as he fed the great sheets of metal into the rolling-mill – the mitten caught and chewed his hand in, to be pulped before the power could be shut off.

No, working wasn't easy, but not working, especially for a long time, was infinitely worse; it led to poverty and loss of worth and dignity. The 'dole' was totally inadequate, and how some of these gallant wives and mothers managed at all I could never understand. They would go to the butcher's and get a bone for soup, shop around for cheap vegetables, and make a great pan of broth . . . that was all they had. I still picture those days in terms of the poor wee 'shilpit' bairns brought for christening. Their mothers were undernourished before they were born. Folk today talk about deprivation if they can't get their forty cigarettes a day. Of course that kind of situation produced cadgers and scroungers, The Public Assistance Office, as it was then called, was opposite the Church; being flung out of there they would seek out the Manse to tell their false or exaggerated tale of woe, backed by some bedraggled infant, probably not their own. My wife, coming in the Church gate from shopping, met just such a couple coming out, just in time to hear the wife say to her husband: 'That was a right soft mark, that was.' She came in blazing for it was true – up to a point you had to be, rather than miss a case of real need. I tried everything; I made an arrangement with the local grocer to honour a line from me for 5s. worth of groceries, in those days quite a lot . . . then I found they were selling them for 4s. You can't win.

Along with another angry young man in the Congregation, Jim Vassie, who went on to be leader writer on economic affairs for the *Scotsman*, we tried to do something more positive. We managed to get possession of a disused malt barn, with a lofty ground floor for the wagons coming in, a low-ceilinged middle floor where the barrels were stored, and a high top floor; we raised by scrounging subscriptions enough money to sponsor a big team of the keener unemployed with their own leaders, shop stewards and the like. Working eagerly they renovated the whole place, creating a combined gym and sports hall on the ground floor; provision for games like draughts, dominoes and chess in the middle; up top we got for the taking away all the tip-up seats from a derelict cinema and made a roomy concert hall. Jim and I cleared out and left the Club in the hands of a Committee of those whose work created it, for it was their show. In a short time we had the police after us for running a gaming club. Did I say 'you can't win'?

Yet all was not doom and gloom in those four years in Bathgate in the early 30s. From September to New Year of our first year I played football for the Bathgate team, another helpful wider contact. Came the Saturday before New Year, I dashed out and dived at the opposing centre forward's feet, and got his boot across my forehead. I went into the pulpit with a suitably liturgical cross on my brow, but made of sticking-plaster. The office-bearers came to me and said: 'We know you got it respectably, but it doesn't look good. We think you had better stop.' So I did. You might say that the 'holy' ordered off the 'goalie'. There was no objection to my playing tennis, which I did all through as one of the Bathgate tennis team; more than half the team were St. John's anyway. I was also deeply involved in Scouting, having founded a Group in St. John's, and also acted as District Commissioner for West Lothian South. The latter involved some grim trips on winter nights up to the moors around bleak spots like Fauldhouse.

Most important of all, during these years our first two children were born in the Manse and therefore qualify as 'Bathgate bairns'. Ronald, born on 14 January 1933, is now Head of the Department of Physical Education in Napier University; Colin, born on 6 September 1935, following in the steps of that famous Bathgate bairn, James Y. Simpson, one of the greatest benefactors of mankind as pioneer of anaesthesia, is now a Senior Consultant Anaesthetist in St. John's Hospital, Livingston, and occasionally puts to sleep some very senior citizen who gets all starry-eyed about these same four years, now so far behind us.

Chapter 6

Kilmarnock pre-War

On 12 December 1935, we moved to the West High Church, Kilmarnock, and the Manse at 25 Glasgow Road, not back to back with the Church as in Bathgate but well over a mile away. I remember it was snowing so hard the removal van could not be unloaded. Jean and I decided we would keep a promise we had made each other while still in Bathgate, namely to share our Christmas dinner with a family where the father had been long unemployed. That first Christmas morning in our new home I took a great pan of broth, a turkey cut in half with all the trimmings, and half a huge Christmas pudding, put them in the car and delivered them to a home in the scheme near us. I went in and found a father and mother and six children sitting round a table covered with newspaper, in the centre a loaf of bread and a packet of the cheapest margarine; the children just stared at the goodies, the parents broke down and wept. With my malt barns scheme, and that shared Christmas dinner, was I just squaring my conscience? Ramsay MacDonald's daughter once said: 'Much of our welfare and caring work is pure aspirin.' Sometimes I wonder.

Kilmarnock, in spite of that not untypical instance, had not been hit quite so hard by the depression. For one thing, its industry was more diversified. We had the great heavy engineering works, Glenfield and Kennedy, who were working on a big contract to make lock gates for a scheme in China; Blackwood Morton carpets, Saxone shoes, Southhook pottery, a locomotive works, and of course, the famous Johnnie Walker. It also had no fewer than sixteen Church of Scotland Churches! Among these the West High held an influential place. It had come out of the Old High at the Disruption, had produced three Moderators and, with a membership double that of Bathgate, was a power in the land. There we settled down to make the most of life in Church and community in the few years of peace that remained.

It was a bit short on youth work so we restarted successfully the 1st Kilmarnock Company of the Boys' Brigade, as that whole area was strongly BB orientated. At the same time I kept my hand in with Scouting as District Commissioner for NE Ayrshire. In that capacity I had to conduct a Memorial Service for Baden Powell when he died in Kenya in 1941. This was held in the Old Parish Church, Stewarton, a typical country Parish Church with outside galleries. As befitted the occasion the ceremonial of the colour parties and presentation of the offering were carefully rehearsed. On the day more of the public than expected turned out, so an outside gallery had to be used. Some idiot gave a Scout patrol leader a bowler hat to take up the Offering. Imagine my chagrin when faced with a solemn procession led by a Scout carrying a bowler hat! We also changed the format of the Bible Class (blackboard and jotters) to a Young People's Fellowship – it must have been one of the earliest – with a membership of 120. Early on, the twelve groups were discussing Youth and the Church, and unanimously reported about the dull hymns, boring Services . . . you never got a chance to say anything till you were too old to have anything worth saying etc., etc. 'All right,' I said, 'I'm calling your bluff. Three months from now you will conduct an entire Morning Service; I will do nothing but pronounce the Blessing.' And they did, beautifully and reverently. They voted on every item and every participant; they produced a choir of thirty and an organist, a beadle, readers, composers and readers of prayers; a girl gave a Children's Address on a piece of coal: 'I am black, but comely'; and a boy and girl each gave a ten minute address on what youth could do in and for the Church . . . it was really most impressive. Of course, all this is 'old hat' these many years but in 1936 it rated a column in the *Daily Express*. Two or three years later most of these youngsters were on Service with the Forces, and several didn't come back. The other great joy was producing a Nativity Play. The tall red-headed boy who had acted beadle was the angel messenger, dressed in his granny's long white nightie with a bit added on; round his neck a string of fairy lights covered with a lace curtain like a scarf. He stepped on stage, I switched him on and he simply glowed. I smelled singeing just in time to switch him off. He is now a Session Clerk.

In the realm of outside interests I joined the Rotary Club, and became its President in 1941. When we moved to Cramond I joined the Edinburgh Club, No. 6 in the British Isles. In 1972 I was President in the 60th Jubilee Year, and am now an Honorary Member, not having to pay dues or keep attendance rules. I have always found it an excellent way of meeting members of other businesses and professions . . . one of my best friends was an Orthodox Jew. In my many travels I have enjoyed temporary associa-

tions with Clubs in other countries. I was Founder President of Kilmarnock
Tennis Club, and played in the team with Tom Campbell, the student who
was abducted from his digs during the rectorial election, by that time
minister of Fenwick. I also resurrected the holy goalie to play for the
ministers and doctors v. the police – the only game I ever played where the
entire crowd were on our side! We won 2-1, the winning goal being scored
by our GP who weighed about nine stone bundling the police goalie, fifteen
stone, ball and all, into the net, to the huge delight of the crowd . . . a
perfectly fair charge. The sequel was that a few weeks later Jimmy
McGrory, ex-Celtic centre forward, then manager of Kilmarnock FC, asked
me to sign as an amateur; he was stuck for a goalie, and as a good RC
didn't mind if he was holy.

One other very happy memory of our earliest years in Kilmarnock. When
we had only Ronald and Colin, both under school age, on a good Monday
in summer we would drive down to Ardrossan and get *The Duchess of
Hamilton* for a day's sail to Inveraray, taking our picnic with us. It was a
glorious day's outing – 5*s.* for adults, under-age children free. Halcyon days
before the storm.

Chapter 7

The War Years

All too soon came the War. Very early on its wastefulness and folly were brought home to us, twice in quick succession. The first death in the Congregation was that of a young soldier, whom I had confirmed and married (and whose two children I had christened), shot by the sentry in some silly larking over the password. The second was a lad who died of a neglected pneumonia in a bleak RAF camp on the Yorkshire moors, neglected by a medical officer who was hardly ever sober . . . how dare you say in a situation like that, *dulce et decorum est, pro patria mori*? In direct contrast was the case of Andrew Muir. Andrew was one of those people who 'clam up' at exams and never do themselves justice, so he was a chemist's assistant, rather than a qualified pharmacist. His young wife died of cancer, leaving him a tiny daughter, Naomi, whom he left with her grandparents when he went off to join the RAF. There he found himself; he was a born flier, won speedy promotion to Squadron Leader and was awarded the DFC. He was grounded after the permitted number of ops. After a raid with heavy casualties, in making up his Squadron for the next raid, he was left with the choice of sending a young, untried pilot or going himself. He chose to go himself, and did not come back. These two contrasting situations seem to me to sum it all up, the sinful waste and the deliberate sacrifice.

For me, personally, the outstanding experience was France, 1940. The Church of Scotland Committee on Huts and Canteens, under the dynamic leadership of Lewis L.L. Cameron, was opening up centres all over north-west France, some in adapted existing buildings and one in a huge new purpose-built hut in the garden of the stationmaster at Amiens, the main railhead for that whole area. On volunteering and getting three months' leave of absence, I was appointed to a team of six (so large was the project): Ronnie Budge (later of Crathie), Jim Donald, David Easton,

31

Bobby Johnston (who had succeeded me in Bathgate), Ian McCulloch and myself. Jim and I went out a few days late, and joined the others the day of the invasion of the Low Countries, when Rotterdam was the first of the great cities to be blitzed. We had a pension to stay in, but the hut itself was hardly usable; only the kitchen and the chapel had both floor and roof – the rest was joists and rafters. On Sunday we went to look for a Protestant Church and found it, typically, in a street out of bounds to British personnel, it had so many houses of ill-fame! We were welcomed by a tall, well-dressed gentleman, the equivalent of the Session Clerk, whose face lit up when he saw the kilt Ian insisted on wearing: 'Ah, you gentlemen are from Scotland . . . so am I. My name is James Carmeechel, and my grandfather came here from Dundee at the end of last century to start the textile business.'

After the Service he insisted on our coming to lunch in his 'little place' which turned out to be an immense chateau; we sat down in two connecting rooms, twenty-five adults in one, twenty-five young people in the other. During lunch he asked if we were needing anything for our canteen; we had to admit we had not even a teaspoon. He turned to his charming daughter and said: 'Marguerite, you will take these gentlemen tomorrow and see about this.' Next day she took us to a huge store that had everything . . . much bowing and scraping by the staff: 'Ah, Mademoiselle Carmeechel, we are honoured' . . . he was the local millionaire, 20% off everything! I remember one purchase out of the many. I asked for '*une urne*' to boil large quantities of tea . . . hilarious mirth . . . I had asked for an urn to put my cremated ashes in! I should have asked for '*une théière*'. Fully supplied with all our purchases we were able during the next week to feed dozens of men who in the prevailing chaos had not eaten for forty-eight hours. The noise of battle came ever nearer, and there had been a lot of bombing, but it was with no sense of urgency that I went next Sunday to the Field Security Police to see if there was any mail. The Major took off: 'Good God, are you people still here? You and we are the only British personnel left, and we're burning documents and getting out; the German tanks will be here any minute. What transport have you got?' Simple answer: 'None.' He offered us a motor bike each, useless with no guarantee of petrol, so he gave us three big army pushbikes, we looted three new ones from a bombed shop, and set out on safari across France.

For a week we travelled in the tide of refugees from Holland, Belgium and north-west France, filling the wide main roads from hedge to hedge, having lost everything. We passed one old woman, all in black, sitting rocking herself by the roadside, and moaning: 'This is the third time this has happened to me' . . . as a young child in the Franco-Prussian War, 1870; as wife and mother in 1914; now as an old granny in 1940. The last time we in Britain suffered that kind of invasion was in 1066. For a week we just went with the tide, being luckier than most, in that we always found somewhere to sleep. The first day we got as far as Rouen, where we had a centre with Roy Sanderson in charge. He managed to get us one room in a hotel with one three-quarter bed for six men. We tossed up, odd man slept on the floor, the other five in the bed criss-cross, like sardines in a tin. On the Sunday of our safari we went to Church, packed with refugees from the Low Countries and north-west France, most of whom had lost everything, singing in Flemish, Dutch, French and English, the German Luther's hymn 'A safe stronghold our God is still'.

We eventually reached Rennes in Britanny, where a number of staff were gathered. For a few days we went around the west coast trying to set up centres. After Dunkirk, which was made to seem quite different from inside France – no one told the French people that their men were being taken off the beaches – it was perfidious Albion once again deserting France. After that it was clear that France was going to collapse, so I drove around, collecting staff from Nantes, St. Nazaire and La Baule, all of us getting out from St. Malo. Just as well, for the next ship out was the *Lancastria* from St. Nazaire . . . she was sunk with very heavy loss of life. It is impossible to describe the difference of atmosphere in landing in Britain from the collapse, military, political, and moral that had taken over in France. It is easy to make fun of the Dad's Army attitude, but it did contribute to what, even in the cynicism of looking back, was our finest hour.

As the time in France was so short, I still had two months of my leave of absence, so I was sent up to Kyle of Lochalsh, which was a subsidiary Fleet Base for mine-laying. There we were serving all three Services: the Camerons guarding the mines in the sidings at Plockton; all the Navy personnel, from the admiral down; and the RAF, manning the balloon barrage that guarded the anchorage. We also had to cater for members of the Services coming off the ferry from Stornoway, often cold and seasick, always hungry. Jean and the family came up and joined me; we stayed in Kyleakin across in Skye. We now had three boys, as Alan had been born in the Manse on 9 May 1937. He later trained for the Ministry and is, in fact, a Licenciate of the Kirk, but chose to go into various forms of Youth Work, and is now an HM Inspector for Community Education. Two memories stand out from these two months. The missionary at Kyle, Mr Munro, had been the last missionary on St. Kilda and his stories of the evacuation disabused us of our romantic notions of simple islanders, unspotted by the world. Jean and I went to a dance in Portree for Service men and women. It was all right for me, I was there in uniform, and it was my job, but the local women did not speak to Jean again: a minister's wife did not go to dances.

After that it was back to Kilmarnock and normal wartime activities. The first of these was comparatively minor. The ministers of the town volunteered to man the telephones in the Report and Control Centre, which was situated in the basement below the public baths . . . a brilliant idea, it only needed a near miss for us all to be drowned. I went on duty at 3.00 a.m., and in the whole War I sent out one red and three yellow alerts. That is the measure of how far Kilmarnock went undamaged. We had one actual raid – one half of a housing scheme block was demolished and the occupants killed, the other half was quite untouched; it looked like a bomber jettisoning his load on the way home from Greenock – most fell in the cemetery. We had in our Hall the refugees from Greenock: 180, mainly mothers and children. Arrangements for reception were chaotic, plenty blankets but no bedding. I tore out the pew cushions from the Church and made one huge bed on the floor. I was besieged by indignant pewholders . . . I had no right, the cushions would need to be cleaned and fumigated. That's the only time in my life I have been really rude to my congregation.

Much more important than the phone duties was my function as Officiating Chaplain to the Forces stationed in and around the town, including AA and searchlight posts around the perimeter, also many units using it as a transit camp. There were experiences grave and gay. I was called out one morning to a searchlight post, to find a man sitting with his head on his hands, utterly shattered. He had just heard that in a heavy raid on Liverpool the night before his home had received a direct hit, and he had lost his parents, wife and children . . . all gone. What could one say? Many of the units were English. When I contacted the colonel of one such, newly arrived, he was delighted and, not having had a Church Parade for some time, gladly arranged it. Then an awful thought struck him and he apologised: 'I'm sorry, padre, of course, I forgot, you will be a Nonconformist,' to which I replied: 'No, sir, you're the Nonconformist.' Another time we had the 1st Royal Scots Fusiliers, a regular battalion, recruited during the depression, largely from Glasgow 'corner boys' . . . great soldiers, but not exactly choice in their vocabulary. They were going overseas, actually to North Africa, and the colonel asked if they could have a farewell Parade in my Church, and, please, could they sing his favourite hymn? I shall never forget that Sunday, the downstairs of the Church filled with soldiers, the congregation crammed into the gallery, and these tough guys belting out the colonel's favourite hymn, especially the second verse . . . 'Shun evil companions, bad language disdain, God's name hold in reverence, nor take it in vain'!

By far the most demanding task was the continuance of my Huts and Canteens involvement, for I supervised all our work in the West of Scotland from Stranraer to Stornoway, including the Inner and Outer Hebrides. This meant a great deal of travel by land, sea and in the air. One beat was by Girvan, Cairnryan, Stranraer, West Freugh, Burrowhead, Wigtown, Kirk-cudbright, Castle Douglas, Thornhill. There were frequent trips to Bute and Arran, or out to Mull, Tobermory, Tiree, then on to Lewis and Harris. The undoubted *pièce de résistance* was a 'recce' to Benbecula, shortly after the steamer *Politician* of *Whisky Galore* fame went ashore. I arrived in time to help to create a local legend. Kate Macdonald, aged eighty-two, was the only inhabitant to rate a funeral where there were two ministers, and all the mourners, having carried her coffin on a hurdle three and a half miles to the ancient burial-ground, redug her sandy grave which had fallen in, and were duly rewarded for their efforts with a whole bottle each.

Perhaps it would be simplest to record at this stage that after the War ended my commitment in this area of Forces Welfare was not 'demobbed' but rather increased. I went on to be Convener of the Committee for twelve years, over the period of BAOR in post-War Germany, National Service, and continuing commitments in the Far East. Shortly after the War ended I visited Austria and Italy, in both of which countries we had busy centres. We did the thing in style, for George Irving, our Area Superintendent, had bought a lovely Rolls Royce for £500 from an Afghan prince who was suffering a cash shortage; this lovely car, with the St. Andrew's Cross on one front wing and the Church of Scotland badge on the other, was very good for the image. Outside the Officers' Club in Florence a group of US officers were positively drooling over 'some automobile' and asked me if I would mind 'switching her on' to which it was my joy to reply nonchalantly: 'she is on.'

Frequent visits to Germany made one realise the appalling devastation; it was estimated that the bomb rubble would build a wall from Hamburg to Munich; this was offset by the incredible determination and industry with which the German people set about rebuilding. One also sensed the sheer inhumanity of the 'non-fraternisation' policy . . . a Tommy, a young father with children of his own was not allowed to give even a piece of his NAAFI ration of chocolate to some pleading-eyed hungry German child; likewise the mad era when the valid currency was cigarettes and some bonnie young mother would sell herself for three cigarettes, having no other way to keep her precious child from starving. Most unforgettable was a trip to Berlin, driving the 120 miles from Helmstedt through the Russian zone, with a queer feeling of threat and dread, profoundly thankful to see the Union Jack at the British check-point for Berlin. It was strange being back after student days in 1929. Three of us visited the Russian Memorial at the Brandenburger Tor and got back into our car, leaving the front passenger seat empty. Suddenly that door opened, a drunk Russian soldier jumped in beside the driver, stuck a revolver in his ear and demanded by signs to be driven to the Russian zone. Fortunately we were stopped at traffic lights just beside a Russian officer; I jumped out and appealed for help. Luckily he understood English, opened the door, twisted the soldier by the ear and led him away . . . to Siberia? It wasn't a nice experience. When eventually the need for this worldwide work had ceased and the Committee was disbanded, I was given the honour of delivering the valedictory in the General Assembly.

It is high time to go back to the ordinary ongoing life of the West High under wartime conditions. We had blacked out the Church from the beginning, and we had for long the only Evening Service, which was a great institution. At 10.00 p.m. I usually went to take a short epilogue at the end of a concert for the Forces in the Corn Exchange. I found the most effective line was not to 'import' a choir but to get the concert party to lead with a familiar sacred solo and a familiar hymn. The two tops of the pops were 'The Holy City' and, after 'Abide with me', 'Cwm Rhonnda'.

During the winter of 1941–42 we ran a series of social evenings for the members in three elders' districts for fellowship and group discussion. After the usual cuppa I read the names of the men and women from the three districts who were away on Service and we had family prayers for them, with special mention of any unusual need. This was much needed and appreciated. The week after the *Prince of Wales* and *Repulse* were sunk off Malaysia we all knew there was no word of Murdoch McKenzie, serving on the *Prince of Wales*, whose parents were at that week's meeting, so we made special mention of him and prayed particularly for him and them, and they were very grateful. After we got home, about 11.00 p.m. I was going to bed when the phone rang. This was Mrs McKenzie to say that they had closed up for the night and were going to bed when the door bell rang. Timid and mystified in the blackout she had opened the door and Murdoch had walked in. He had been picked up by a Chinese junk, and after a week got where he could be sent home, with no chance to inform them.

All through the War I was continually amazed at the courage, endurance and faith of ordinary people. There were sadly many losses, borne with great fortitude, and long periods of heartbreaking anxiety. Typical was Mrs

Johnston, with eighteen of a family, and six sons away and in danger, on land, at sea and in the air. I once asked her how she stood it all and she said: 'Sometimes it comes over me all of a sudden, waiting for a bus or standing in the queue in a shop. I just shut my eyes and pray: "Dear Lord, help me to go on" and He always does.'

On the purely domestic front these years brought special events. Outstanding was the birth, after three boys and a gap of six years, of our daughter, Catriona. She was born in the Burgh Maternity Home on 29 August 1943, at 7.40 on what was a Sunday evening. The time in this case is important, because the next week a fellow-member at a meeting in '121' (121 George Street, Edinburgh, the headquarters of the Church of Scotland) said to me: 'That was very dramatic the way you announced your daughter's birth from the pulpit.' I said: 'What on earth do you mean?' 'Yes,' he replied, 'You were in the middle of your sermon when the beadle climbed up the pulpit steps, whispered to you, and you turned to the congregation and said: "My wife has just had a daughter . . . God be praised" and went on and finished your sermon.' In fact Catriona was not born till ten minutes after the Service ended.

Even that happy event was overshadowed by the War. Among the young men of the Congregation with whom I was specially friendly was a lad, John Strang. We had long talks, and he unburdened his soul . . . he was a navigator cum bomb aimer in the RAF, and he hated what he had to do, pressing the release and sending death and destruction, without distinction, inevitably on women and children below . . . it was his grim duty, but he still hated it. The night that Catriona was born he went on a raid over Duisburg and was shot down. His father, who was a jeweller, gave me a lovely gold watch, suitably inscribed, in memory of my friendship with John. That, too, was stolen when my football medal was taken.

As the year ended and we moved forward into 1944, it began to be clear that the tide of battle had definitely turned, and that to leave would not be deserting one's post, and as D-Day drew near we began to prepare for the move to Cramond. We were truly sorry to be leaving Kilmarnock, for these years had been very special. Our family was now complete; the boys had begun school-life at Kilmarnock Academy; they had also become familiar with farm-life, with their constant visits to Toponthank Farm, a mile away, with their school pals John and Willie Cuthbertson, the farmer's sons. Jean had gained greatly from sharing all the wartime activities with the women of the church and community, while I had undergone sundry adventures without taking any hurt, and had learned much from meeting all sorts of people, and coping with challenging situations. Yes, the Kilmarnock years did much to prepare and fit us for what we had still to do.

Chapter 8

Cramond

Moving to Cramond was a major undertaking, fraught with all sorts of problems. Affecting everything was the fact that the War was still on; it was July after D-Day. There had been a badly muddled and mishandled vacancy which had lasted almost two years, with the inevitable deterioration in the general situation. The state of the Manse and garden was off-putting to say the least. The grass, which constituted a considerable portion of the near two and a half acres, had grown through, died back, and grown through again, so was a tangled mass. We got the local dairy farmer to go over it with his hay-cutter, and we had the Presbytery tea among the hayricks on the lawn! There was no petrol for a motor mower, and an afternoon's toil with a hand mower, jamming every few pushes with stringy roots, cleared no more than about five square yards. Every known form of persistent weed had taken over, convolvulus, bishop weed, rack etc. In the event it took Alex the beadle and myself years to get it back to normal, mainly by double digging. There were two prestigious Golf Clubs in the Parish, Royal Burgess and Bruntsfield, both of whom said that as Parish minister I could play any time I liked. In twelve years I played five and a half rounds . . . I was a compulsive gardener!

The Manse had been empty for the same time, and was not an easy building to begin with, built in three different centuries, with stone stairs, a basement kitchen, old black iron fireplaces; the bedroom windows had been left open at the top to let air in; the swallows had got in and nested round the cornices . . . the mess can be imagined. When Jean and I went through, we were taken to see the Church first, or we would never have gone; after being shown over the Manse we went back to Kilmarnock and never spoke to each other. However, after the wartime building restrictions were lifted, improvements were made and we spent twelve of the happiest years of our lives in that same Manse, and came to enjoy and appreciate our garden.

Churchwise, too, things were difficult. There had not been any Evening Service for several years, there was a tiny Sunday School, and similar Woman's Guild, and any youth work had been wiped out by the War. We started an Evening Service in the Hall at Davidson's Mains which was immediately popular; I set up a Scout Troop with eleven boys in the little Primary School. One of the problems was that there was no accommodation at the Church except the small Offertory House, at the gate. Later this lack became acute. Meantime I had transferred my Officiating Chaplain's duties to Scottish Command at Craigiehall, and Sunday began at 9.30 with a Service; out of that came a group of eight ATS girls who wanted to join the Church. They came to the Preparation Class in the Manse, always in the charge of Sergeant Jenny Davidson to make sure they didn't skive off and go somewhere else. At the end, when they had all decided to go through with it, I said to Jenny: 'Jenny, you've been through it all like the rest; what about you?' 'Och! padre,' she replied, 'You should know you canna be a Sergeant in the ATS and a Christian at the same time!' 'Well,' I said, 'You could have a jolly good try' and she did. A few years later I had a letter

Victory Parade in Mall, 1946 (RLS in file third from front, next to saluting base)

from Jenny from Los Angeles, married and clearly well into the life of the Church there, enclosing several dollars for the Kirk, and a wee message . . . 'still having a jolly good try!' I have quoted Jenny to quite a few folk who made her original excuse.

The War ended the next year; VE Day was duly celebrated by the ringing for fifteen minutes of the old bell, cast by Michael Burghersdyk in 1619. This famous bell was carried off to London by General Monk's soldiers in 1656 and, after strong protest, returned five years later, which has been quoted as a record for getting a return from London! Our three boys helped Alex to ring, all laying on the rope so heartily that they turned it off the pulley and had to push it to ring the rest of the fifteen minutes. With the men and women coming back from the Forces, settling down, bringing up their families, the place simply took off. Accommodation became an urgent problem. In early September I intimated that a class for children under five would meet in the basement kitchen of the Manse, and forty-four children crowded in. We had to have accommodation; we got a building permit for a contractor to lay the cement floor of a hall in the Manse garden. We bought an RAF hut from Earlston; it was nominally 'sectional' but, being made of plaster board, it was in assorted pieces; however we rebuilt it with two squads of volunteers – retired men during the day, other men after work in the evening.

The large number of christenings also created a problem; after crowding six babies plus adults into a tiny vestry, we built on instead a beautiful large Session House, the builders complaining they couldn't get their foundations for walls left by the Romans, of whom more anon. A different kind of problem arose out of the same phenomenon . . . return from the Forces. We had started a Young People's Fellowship for the 16-18 year olds and it was flourishing; then came a tremendous influx of different young folk, still in their early 20s; they had been commanding bombers, tanks, tank landing craft etc., and they could not mix with such a young group, nor could they be expected to. After about three uneasy joint meetings the senior group hived off and founded the Young People's Association which they ran themselves, happily, imaginatively and efficiently.

Another new departure which functioned happily was Open Air Services at the riverside on summer Sunday evenings. There was a spot, roughly where Columban monks from Inchcolm were reputed to have landed, with a wide stretch of ground backed by a grassy bank. We set up a portable organ and folding forms, and we had in fact three congregations: those who occupied the forms and stood close around; the young folk who sat on the grass bank; and people walking their dogs along the front, embarrassed to find themselves mixed up in a religious Service, walking past, then stopping and listening from the shelter of the shrubbery. Forty years later I heard of one such dog-walker, a professing atheist, who came to every Service of that summer, and in the autumn joined the Church!

This may be a suitable point at which to refer to a not dissimilar activity in which I became involved in those post-War years. There was a technique in modern evangelism developed in England near the end of the War, mainly by the Methodist Church, called a Christian Commando Campaign. The principle was to go wherever people would receive you and allow you a hearing: cinemas, pubs, works canteens, shops, offices etc. I had taken part in one in London, and in 1947 a similar one was held in Edinburgh, with myself as joint leader with Morrison Neilson of the Methodist Central Hall. We had a large team of many denominations with a strong experienced contingent from over the border. We went into all sorts of places – I was in every pub in Leith Walk! We were everywhere received with kindness and given an appreciative hearing.

One particular memory still stands out. We were doing the briefing meeting in the morning for a visit to the Palais de Dance in Fountainbridge, which was then a very posh place for parties. The leader really picked himself, because we had a little chap who was rector of Spennymoor and who had been a music hall artist and had a perfect command of the required technique. Along with him we chose a large team to go and sit in with the dancers at the tables. After all this was arranged, a mild looking elderly gentleman came and said to me, 'You haven't given me any allocation.' 'Where would you like to go?' I said. 'To the Palais de Dance,' he replied. 'Right, just go and join the team.' This I said, hiding with difficulty my impression that this was an unsuitable posting. To the Palais de Dance they went; the band leader announced, 'Let's give a big hand to the Christian Commando team,' which the dancers did heartily. Our music hall artist did his stuff to perfection, and the rest of the team sat in at the tables. My elderly gentleman found himself sitting beside the band leader who turned out to be a Muslim. And it also turned out that my elderly (unsuitable) gentleman had just retired after teaching for thirty years in a school in what was to become Pakistan – teaching Muslims! And we sometimes have the nerve to imagine that God doesn't know what He is doing! In 1950 we held a similar campaign in Glasgow, with the same kind of reception, and at least one other 'coincidence'.

Quite early on we were confronted with an unexpected problem – I was inducted in July 1944, and got no stipend until November 1945! This was because my predecessor, Dr Stott, had been in office before 1929, and had a life interest which could not be interfered with. Cramond was therefore one of the few parishes in Scotland still on the unstandardised teind stipend. I had experienced the other methods of payment; in the UP Church the stipend was paid a quarter in advance – indeed, the Presbytery clerk had to see and certify that it was, in fact, paid on the day of the Induction! In the Free Church part was paid, monthly, 'backhanded', the rest went to the Central Fund in '121' and the balance came back later. The teind stipend set-up was much more complicated and, seeing it is now so much a thing of the past, it may be useful if I just outline what happened.

After a vesting date in summer, which we had just missed, a schedule was sent in September to every farmer in Midlothian, requiring him to enter all sales to the end of the year of the following . . . 1st. 2nd. 3rd. barley, ditto, wheat and oats, peas and beans, with the weight, the price, and the purchaser. Knowing what most farmers are like in the keeping of records, many returns were 'inspired guesses'; even so they were all brought together at the beginning of the year and submitted to the Scrutinising Committee, consisting of Mr Herdman, a farmer, Mr Douglas, a miller, 'Micky' Dempster and myself. Those that passed muster were then handed to the actuaries to do their abstruse calculations. Finally, the Fiars Court met in February with the Sheriff Principal in the chair. He put the actuary, the miller and the farmer on oath (he must have trusted the parsons), and took their evidence on the accuracy of the price suggested for each of the commodities under the conditions prevailing that year. He asked for comments from the kirk . . . we always pointed out that with the system of grants and subsidies this did not represent the total payment the farmer received for his crops. This was always duly noted, but nothing was done.

The Sheriff then declared the Fiars price for each commodity, then back to the actuaries to calculate that Mr X was occupying, say, half an acre of land in the Parish of Cramond on which barley had been grown and was liable for stipend of £YZ. Some sums were so small that they just had to be written off; organisations like the Merchant Company were liable for considerable amounts. Only when it had all been collected could it be paid out, three-tenths to Dr Stott as his pension, seven-tenths to me as stipend. With all this to go through, my first payment came in November 1945; till then I was given a loan from the Maintenance of the Ministry Fund. When Dr Stott died his widow, under the Law of Ann, got the whole stipend for six months . . . after that I got it all. Such was the system which had prevailed in the old Parish Church for centuries. There were also some strange survivals of payments in kind. The Parish Minister of North

Berwick was entitled to twenty-four solan geese off the Bass Rock, and when I moved to St. Cuthbert's I became entitled to all the fish out of the Nor' Loch!

Meantime Church life in Cramond was going like a fair. Special Church buses brought people out from town; we had to instal extra pews to fold up like shelves on brackets. The Youth Work had developed widely and was very active, with Cubs, Scouts, Brownies, Guides . . . the lot. As Group Scoutmaster I had great fun. We got from the Corps of Signals a lorry-load of stout poles which they had used as telephone poles; we cut them up and

Jean . . . at her best

used them for bridge-building, which became our speciality. At one Parents' Night in the Manse garden we started with poles and lashings carefully laid at the side of the drive opposite the front door, I blew the whistle, the Scouts started to build two piers with supports and main bearers, and thirty minutes later the Troop marched out of the door and over the bridge while I drove the car underneath. Talk about chancing your luck! The beauty of it was that all the youngsters were in everything together; the hub of the universe on a Friday night was Mrs Poustie's chip shop in Davidson's Mains.

It was a great place for the family to grow up, with the river, the boats and the countryside. After a brief period at the little local Primary School the boys got into George Watson's. Catriona, who was only ten months old when we came to Cramond, spent the first twelve happy years of her life there. Very early on she was 'adopted' by Alex Dalrymple, the beadle. 'Akit' as the wee thing called him, was a great character . . . a recently retired blacksmith who could do anything. She went everywhere with him, helped him to do everything, whether it was cleaning the Church or digging the graves! It got quite embarrassing . . . she would come in with a bunch of fresh flowers, and we never knew which grave she had taken them from. One day she brought in an alabaster angel: 'Bonnie babba, Mummy, bonnie babba!' After her first years of schooling, she went to Cranley, whose headmistress, Miss Porteous, had been at Lothian Road with Jean. To continue her story, she then went on to train in domestic science at Atholl Crescent, and now works part time in Watson's cookery department. Her husband, Graham Young, is sales manager for Kellys of Bonnyrigg, who specialise in catering equipment for schools, hospitals etc. She chose him with great foresight for, having played rugby for Watsonians and Scotland, he is now one of the Scottish selectors, which brings all sorts of 'perks' to the lass who started her career of acquiring blessings with an alabaster angel off a Cramond grave!

Chapter 9

Special Occasions

On the last day of 1949, when we had been five and a half years in Cramond, I received an unusual and exciting letter. It was from the Session Clerk of Knox Church, Dunedin, New Zealand, explaining that, being faced with a long vacancy, they had asked Principal John Baillie to suggest some young man who might go out for five months as Guest Preacher, and he had suggested myself. It was a most attractive proposition – all travelling and living expenses for Jean and myself, plus adequate funds to cover all costs of any replacement in Cramond – but at first sight it was clearly impossible in view of all the commitments I had in the 7-8 months that would be needed, including travelling time, especially as we would be arriving back just a few days before the start of the Glasgow Commando Campaign, to which I have referred, and which I was to lead. Next day, New Year's Day 1950, we went to first foot my parents, now living in Corstorphine, and I showed the letter to my father, by then in his late 80s. His immediate reaction was: 'What a splendid idea! When do you leave?' He demolished all my arguments as to its impossibilities, and by 1 March we were away, leaving Cramond in charge of Prof. Willie Tindal, and the family in the tender and loving care of dear Granny McGregor.

In spite of all the wartime restrictions still in operation, (including rationing) we managed to get a cabin on the P & O liner *Stratheden* to Sydney; from there we were stuck. One of my Cramond elders, Ernest Watt, happened to be a director of Distillers Company. He asked me how our travel plans were going, and I told him of this problem – he said he would see what he could do. Next Sunday he came and told me we had booked a cabin on the *Wanganella*, Sydney to Auckland. When I asked how this had been managed, he replied: 'Our people in Sydney got on to the shipping line, who responded: 'A case of your whisky for the captain's cabin, and the berths are yours.' So here was I, Convener of the Temperance Committee,

45

almost literally floated off on whisky! (This theme will recur quite soon.)

Anyhow, we floated off from Tilbury and, to begin with, as we steamed south from the cold of March, it was wonderful just to sit and relax after the rush of getting away, to choose from a full menu, and have no guilty conscience. After two weeks however I had had enough of the idleness and inanity of shipboard life, relieved only by deck games, religiously walking round the deck to keep fit – 17 times round = 1 mile – or the idiotic horse-racing in the evening; I decided I would never make a cruis-er. Fortunately we had congenial company. We were in charge of Christine, the vivacious younger sister of Jim Matheson, then minister of St. Columba's, Blackhall, who will appear prominently in our ongoing saga at a later stage. We were taking her to Bombay to marry Carmy Clark, who had played football at University with Jim and me. There was also a girl Macarthur, related to an Iona family, who was going to Adelaide. We had great fun kidding on our table steward which was the wife. I did not wear my clerical collar till the morning we were docking at Bombay, for ease of recognition. At breakfast that morning the steward handed me the menu, took one look at the collar, beat his brow and exclaimed: 'Oh! my God! what have I been saying?'

Our first port of call was at Port Faud, at the north end of the Suez Canal – frantic waving from the dockside to come ashore for breakfast. This was Alan Anderson, a Cramond member, wartime submarine Commander, officer on Shaw Savill *Dominion Monarch* and now a canal pilot. His family from Davidson's Mains had recently joined him, and it was fun, sitting in a house in Egypt, with the same pictures on the walls. When we rejoined the ship we could hardly get into the cabin for flowers – it was like film star treatment – and a card 'With the Compliments of Sir William Cowan'. 'Who on earth's Sir William?' I asked the cabin steward, who was obviously much impressed by our posh connections. Shocked by my ignorance, he replied: 'Don't you know? He's the Chairman of P & O' – he was also Chairman of DCL, hence the flowers. The final touch came when we got to Sydney when, for our two days there, DCL supplied a car, chauffeur and guide. By the way, I discovered the origin of the word 'posh' which I have just used. Booking for a voyage to the Far East influential people would specify: 'Port outwards . . . starboard homewards', thus keeping on the shady, therefore cooler, side of the ship each way – hence PO SH!

We called next at Aden in blazing heat; the Arabs came out in their bumboats and threw up a clothes rope, which prospective purchasers tied to the rail; goods were pulled up in a shopping basket 'on approval' and typical eastern bargaining went on. There was a Glasgow woman who had the patter to a T, so much so that the rest got her to do their bargaining for them. A group of Americans from First Class were spectating . . . they understood every word of the Arabs but not one from the 'Glesca buddy'! The next stop was Bombay which, after all these years, I cannot recall without a shudder. It is the only time and place I have had to step over people lying dying in the street; it was so soon after the partition of India that refugees from Pakistan were still flooding in and all the welfare services were overwhelmed; the ledges of the banks, insurance offices etc. were all filled with bodies for whom, apparently, nothing could be done. One was reminded how often decisions are taken for political reasons at top level which mean death and disaster for men, women, and pathetic children 'at the grass roots'. What made it even worse was the fact that, not far away on Malabar Hill, there were more millionaires to the square mile than anywhere else outside America.

From there, ever southward, ever hotter, to Colombo and the Scots Kirk, where the minister was Taylor McKenzie who had succeeded my father in North Berwick, and who was married to Isobel Eason, daughter of the Session Clerk in the Abbey Church. The famous 'spicy breezes' must have been having their day off, for it was very hot. We actually played tennis – mad dogs and Scotsmen! A long leg from there across the Indian Ocean brought us to Fremantle, where Jean, homesick for her family, nearly 'jumped ship' to a homeward bound liner just leaving as we docked. We had our first, brief sight of the lovely city of Perth. The Bay of Biscay, even in March, had been unusually kind, and the great Australian Bight, with a similar reputation, let us gently through to Port Melbourne, where four families met us, each demanding we come home with them. We compromised and took in two with a party in both. The name on the gate of the first was Pilrig, for the Nelsons had met in Princes Street and married in Pilrig Church – she was the sister-in-law of a Cramond elder. The second night we stayed at Dunblane. From there to Sydney by train, getting out at Albury in the middle of the night to change trains – different gauges because of the silly rivalry and jealousy between States! At Sydney, because of the laziness of the dockers one of our trunks failed to be transferred to the *Wanganella*, so we sailed on her for Auckland without my robes and sermons – it was six weeks before I got them. We ran into a dreadful storm on the Tasman Sea, so bad that there were only thirty out of three hundred down to breakfast, including Jean and me. A lone passenger opposite us at the long table ordered three kippers, ate one, turned green, went out and was sick, came back and ate the other two. That finished us! Happily we sailed into Auckland harbour on calm seas, and that Easter Day was a real Thanksgiving Service.

From Auckland we travelled by overnight train to Wellington, where we stayed for a day with Bill Temple, who had come out from the Barclay Church, Edinburgh. He had been a member of the famous Ministers' Concert Party, started in our Kilmarnock days, with Bill, violinist; Tom Morton, tenor; Willie McIntyre, bass; Jack Prendergast, solo piano and accompanist; and myself, compère. We had raised a lot of money for good causes and had a lot of fun. Next day, ferry to Picton, then Christchurch, which is a beautiful, very 'English' city, centring round an Anglican Cathedral, with the river Avon running through it, and suburbs like St. Albans, where the first of Jean's many aunts, uncles, cousins etc. lived. Unfortunately for those who get all starry-eyed and Shakespearean, the original settlement was a farm called Riccarton, owned by Scots brothers called Deans, and the Avon is a burn in Ayrshire – so the Scots were there first.

Mention of Jean's relatives makes it necessary to explain that her maternal grandfather, George Law, was a crofter-blacksmith, in a tiny place in north Aberdeenshire called Cobairdy. He and all the family, except two daughters already married, emigrated in 1913 – the others were to follow, but the War stopped all that. The family settled in Waimate. George, the eldest son, married Charlotte, or Chat, a young girl they had taken with them to help with the younger children on the voyage, and a kind of dynasty grew up. It is typical that, going into successive generations from that humble, hardworking couple, have come doctors, nurses, chemists, scientists, teachers, sheep farmers – all with the old Scots idea that, if you want something worthwhile, you work to get it. The old man was still singing in the choir of the Presbyterian Church when he was ninety-three! On the way to Dunedin we stayed with several of the families. Cousin Ngairi Hurst was married to Ian, a sheep farmer; he had a small place, just 69,000 acres, mostly hill, on which he ran 3,000 sheep. We were told to stay in bed for breakfast, and Ngairi brought me a huge meat-plate with two mutton chops, two fried eggs, two sausages, four rashers of bacon, and two spoonfuls of mashed potatoes! That was a normal breakfast for a man – they killed a sheep every two days, cut it in half, ate one half themselves and hung up the other half for the dogs. And we marvel at the upper body strength of the All Blacks! When we got to Waimate, I christened a great-grandson for good measure. And so to journey's end and Dunedin.

Once we had arrived and settled into our flat on the corner of Pitt Street and London Street, we took the tram to the terminus at Opoho, and started to climb Signal Hall, which looks down on Dunedin as Arthur's Seat does on Edinburgh. The climb was steep and long; we were very hot, and wondered if it was worth going on, but we did, and it was.

Let into the top of the hill, with no connection with its geological surroundings was a boulder with this inscription:

This boulder from the Castle Rock of Edinburgh, Scotland, was sent to Dunedin in 1948, to commemorate the longstanding bonds of friendship between the two Cities.

We just stood and wept buckets – we were so homesick.

The City is very Scottish, founded as it was, a Free Church foundation from Edinburgh . . . indeed, Dunedin is the Gaelic equivalent of Edinburgh. The co-founders were a lawyer called Cargill, a descendant of Donald Cargill, the Covenanting preacher executed at the Grassmarket, and the Rev. James Burns, who was the nephew of Robert Burns . . . you can work out the genes of that joint heritage. Burns had been minister of Regent Street Free Church, Portobello, so the suburbs are Portobello, Mussel-burgh, Waverley, and a very posh place, pronounced Córstorphíne, with the accent on the first syllable! They landed at Port Chalmers, named for the founder of the Free Church; they bought millions of acres from the Maoris and, while they were still living in mud huts, set aside great tracts of land for two typical Scottish purposes – to build Churches and to build a University. The University of Otago is a kind of compromise: the building is modelled on that of Glasgow, but it stands on the Water of Leith, and like Edinburgh, it is famed for its Medical School.

This transporting of Scots names is widespread – central Otago, famed for fruit growing, is Ettrick and Teviotdale, with names like Roxburgh, Heriot and Peebles; down in the south, Invercargill (origin obvious) has every street named from a Scottish river or burn. Dunedin itself centres round a statue of Robert Burns in Moray Place, and the Church where we were to serve for five months was Knox Church . . . here we go again. We travelled around a lot, seeing that lovely country. Of special interest was a trip down south as far as Stewart Island, which lies off the south of New Zealand as Orkney lies off the north of Scotland. We stayed the night in Invercargill and crossed next morning from the port of Bluff. The date was 1 August – if we had been at home, we would have sailed from Oban and landed at Iona. That day we landed at Oban, climbed the hill above it and looked down on the island of Iona! We spent the day with a retired woman missionary from the New Hebrides. I still remember the lovely Maori name of her home, Maikarewoana, which means 'I dreamed a dream'. During the day she said to me: 'It's Edinburgh you come from, isn't it?'

I replied: 'Well, it's really an old village, going back to Roman times, called Cramond.'

'Cramond . . . Cramond . . . is there a place at Cramond with a funny name, like "Fairy-fa" or "Fair-a-far"?'

'Yes, there's a place called "Fair-a-far".'

'Is there a farm there?'

'Yes, there's a farm,' (which was true then, but not now).

'That's funny,' she went on, 'I used to have a grand aunt who was the wife of the farmer at Fair-a-far – a Mrs Lawrie – she must be dead long ago.'

'Well, she wasn't dead when she knitted the socks I'm wearing at this moment!'

Apart from all these interesting experiences, the growing central feature of our life in Dunedin was what was happening in Knox Church. From quite early on attendances began to build up. Soon the Morning Service was full; but it was the Evening that was the surprise and inspiration. The students began to come in ever-increasing numbers; people began to queue one and a half hours before the Evening Service. On my very first Sunday the beadle, a typical exiled Scot, put me properly in my place:

'I can mind o' the great days in this Kirk. Years ago we had a famous preacher out from London, and it got that the Kirk was that thrang there were folk sitting on the pulpit steps; but that's a' by wi' noo, thae days'll never come again.'

When things were really 'hotting up', the beadle aforesaid was late in coming round after ringing the bell. He came in, shut the door firmly behind him, and addressed me thus:

'Ye mind on your first day I tellt ye about the great days when the Kirk was crowded, and warned you that thae daes would never come again? Well, by God, they've came. When I open that door into the pulpit you watch it. Ye'll hae to climb over folk tae get in.'

It just went on building up, till there was an overflow of three hundred in the Sunday School Hall. I had been doing a series on the Apostles' Creed, taking more than one evening to great phrases like 'His Only Son, our Lord' . . . it worked out that we had to extend our stay by a week, otherwise they would have been left without 'the life everlasting'. As it worked out that the last Evening Service was broadcast, most of the Churches throughout the South Island put a loudspeaker in the pulpit and took in the Service.

It was a difficult situation to handle. As Hugh Douglas was to say of the adulation sometimes offered to the Moderator: 'It's all right, as long as you don't inhale!' It was a 'preacher's dream of paradise'. The net result was that we were under extreme pressure to go back for good. We sailed from Wellington on an old Shaw Savill liner, the *Mataroa*, going home to be broken up. Night after night she chugged across the Pacific at fifteen knots, and we sat on the top deck and wrestled with our problem – one moment we were trying to decide what furniture to take with us, the next we were agreeing that it was not fair to commit the family to becoming New Zealanders, which probably would have happened – there was never any clear guidance. Night after night a solitary albatross swung poised overhead; I would have cheerfully shot it, so calm, in control of its situation. After ten days we called in, excitingly, at Pitcairn Island, and the descendants of the mutineers on the *Bounty* came out to sell us their baskets and other goods – I always remember their huge bare feet.

So finally we landed and went ashore at Colon. This was still the era when nylons had been for years unknown and ladies were painting their legs and drawing an imitation 'seam' with a biro. Jean found a shop offering gift wrapped, five pairs of nylons for £10, which she clutched protectively to her bosom. On returning to the ship we were at once engrossed in the entry to the Canal. The ship was moored to the electric 'mules' – small locomotives running on a rack railway – four each side, till she was held firmly in a kind of web; some 6 million gallons of water were pumped into the huge lock; the gates ahead were opened after she had been lifted several feet when the mules moved her forward on the new level; this was thrice repeated till her thousands of tons had been raised from the level of the Pacific to the Gatun Lakes. This thrill over, we retired to our cabin to gloat over the nylons. There wasn't a pair in the package or one you could make up – there were tiny feet for Chinese women, huge feet for the Pitcairn women – Jean had been done, good and proper. We chugged on across the Caribbean, stopping for oil at Curaçao, where Jean found a $10 bill in the ladies' powder-room, and shamelessly kept it as compensation.

And so to Southampton, London and home. We had sailed round the world and seen many famous places and beauty spots; as we drove along Princes Street the Castle was floodlit for the Festival; we looked at each other and with one voice declared: 'This is the nicest, loveliest place we've been in yet.' Even when we were home and reunited with the family, and Churchwise back to normal, there was no clear guidance. I asked advice from many knowledgeable friends, and was no clearer. I went to Glasgow and got caught up in the demands of the Commando Campaign. Came

Friday and I knew that by lunchtime I had to cable my final decision to Dunedin and I still did not know what it was going to be. At midday I was sitting with the team on the platform in a big works canteen – suddenly it came to me: 'It is in this country and with Scots folk that you belong' – I went straight out and cabled Dunedin, and never had a twinge of regret. Talk about the Lord waiting to the eleventh hour – that was the fifty-ninth minute of the eleventh hour. Maybe someone reading these words needs the message I was given.

Knox Church accepted my refusal with a good grace, and proceeded to appoint a commission to choose a minister from Scotland, whom they undertook to accept. The commission was composed of John Baillie and Archie Craig for their wisdom and experience, plus myself, for my recent knowledge of the situation. John Baillie, as convener, suggested we should each make up our list in order of priority, then meet at his house and compare notes, which we did.

'Archie, who's first in your list?'

'Jim Matheson of St. Columba's, Blackhall.'

'Leonard?'

'Jim Matheson, of St. Columba's, Blackhall.'

The Principal looked almost nonplussed for a moment, then said:

'Strange – he's first on my list, too. No further argument needed?'

I was then deputed to sell the idea to Jim, whose vivacious sister, Christine, we had taken out to Bombay to get married. He duly went out, and had an influential ministry in Knox Church for some nine years. During that time he became deeply involved in the Christian Stewardship Movement, which developed in New Zealand before it did in Scotland. When the Stewardship and Budget Committee's work was becoming important enough to merit and indeed demand a full-time Secretary, I happened to be the Convener, and proposed the appointment of Jim Matheson, which was accepted, in the light of his special experience. It then fell to me to nominate him to the Commission of Assembly who duly appointed him. So, having sent him to New Zealand, I also brought him back. He played such a valuable and honoured part in the work of the Church that he went on to become Moderator.

The other special occasion took us in the opposite direction, back across the Atlantic to America. In 1952 I had a phone call from South Carolina, and in those days that was a momentous event. This was from a Presbyterian minister, Bill Ward, in the city of Spartanburg. He had been for a term at New College, and had frequented Cramond . . . he now wanted to bring his wife and two young sons to share the pleasure he had found in

Scotland, and particularly in a place like Cramond, so different from anything he had known in his own country. Would I consider exchanging for, say four months, Church, Manse etc.? He had a friend who was then at New College and coming to Cramond, who helped to work out the details of what was then a quite new idea. In the event they arrived just before we left, so there was a few days' overlap, including a Sunday. Cramond possesses a rare first edition of the Authorised Version, dated 1611, with ancient spelling and letters like a woodcut; we got Bill to read the Lessons from it and he was thrilled.

This time we took the family; five and a half fares were a bit of an economic gamble, but in the end it amply paid off; we crossed on the *Queen Mary* which was a great experience. After one night in New York we went down by Greyhound bus, which was cheaper, and stopped off for a night with friends who had a Cramond connection in Washington DC. Next morning back on the bus – the air-conditioning broke down so we drove the remaining hundreds of miles in stifling heat. In fact the heat was the inescapable reality of our stay. The day we arrived in Spartanburg the temperature was 97°F, in Cramond 57°F. The difference for us Scots was that we were so far from the sea. It has been said that there is nowhere in Scotland you can be more than fifty miles from salt water, as the seagull flies; if you count in the sea lochs running deep into the land, that is probably true. We were far from the sea, part of a huge land mass, and of course in the Deep South. There was no air-conditioning then in Manse or Church. In the Manse we coped by shutting all doors and windows first thing in the morning, opening and shutting as quickly as possible – don't let the heat in. You watched the thermometer on the verandah; in the early evening when it showed a downward trend, then the not colder but less hot air was coming down from the mountains – you opened everything, put on the big extractor fan in the attic and sucked the hot air out. When it came to sleeping we put five beds on the great sleeping porch, where the temperature was a few degrees lower than in the bedroom. That was when I said the children were like the ancient Israelites – they slept with their fathers.

When I entered their lovely Church on Sunday I was moved by the welcome: they were all waving to me – actually waving their palm-leaf fans to keep themselves cool. I was the only person in the building without a fan. There were other lovely ways of keeping cool; the family spent most of their time in beautiful private pools, while Dad was being trailed round the hospitals from 10.00 a.m. by the Pastoral Assistant. People were very good, too, at inviting us out for a few days to their cabin on one of the lakes, for swimming, canoeing, water ski-ing and the like. Indeed, the hospitality was almost overpowering – the first fourteen times we were invited out for an evening meal we were given Southern fried chicken! Some things surprised us, such as the widespread ignorance about Scotland and the Scots. One of my first outside engagements was to speak at the Conference of the Women of the Church at the Assembly Centre at Montreat, North Carolina, where Billy Graham has his holiday home. Catriona was at the Speakers' Table with us; the three boys were at a table by themselves, wearing their kilts – Murray, McGregor and Lindsay tartans. The waitresses, all College girls doing a job in the vacation, gathered round them chattering away. Suddenly the three boys burst out laughing at something they found very funny. When they came over afterwards, I asked: 'What were you lot laughing at?'

'Well,' said Ronald, 'one of those girls, a second year University student, said to us: "You speak English very well . . . how long have you been speaking it?"'

Church life surprised us, first by its obvious wealth – they had a paid staff of seventeen and had just completed building a set of halls and rooms to complete the square of their 'plant'. This left them short of pianos, so they just bought eight new ones! The other thing was a lack of reverence – at the Morning Service people drifted in any time during the first half hour. Jean and I went to a famous Bible Conference at Massanetta Springs in Virginia. The first morning Jean went to the Women's Meeting, chaired by the wife of the President of the Conference, a charming, cultured lady. In her opening devotions she prayed: 'O Lord, we thank you that we were able to get away to this Conference with an easy mind – we had time to defrost the frig and air and put away the baby's diapers.' A Welsh speaker told me he had heard a pastor pray, the previous year: 'O Lord, as you no doubt read about yourself this morning in the *New York Times* . . .'!

Another worry arose from the expressions of colour bar. They had two negro janitors, Izzy (Isaiah) and Jerry (Jeremiah); they were in the Church every day, lovingly cleaning and polishing, but they were not allowed into the Service on Sunday. I was asked, early on, to preach in the coloured folk's Church, and at once agreed. I was pressurised by the ministers of the town not to go: 'It will be interpreted as being the attitude of the Church of Scotland.' I replied: 'That is exactly why I am going,' and I went. The singing was tremendous, led by a grand piano, splendidly played by a tall, rather gaunt black lady, to whom I was afterwards introduced: 'Dr Small, this is Miss Georgina Campbell.' Having no right to names of their own, the emancipated slaves took the name of their last owner – in this case clearly an exiled Scot. It was a new experience to have behind me on the platform a

ring of negro pastors providing a kind of obbligato: 'Praise the Lord . . .
Amen . . . Hallelujah . . .'

That brings me to their special Services. The first 'infant baptisms' I had
were a boy and girl, both two and a half, which was the norm. When I took
the lovely little blue-eyed blondie in my arms, she swung her arm, and hit
me a shot on the face that rang through the Church . . . and they say that
American girls are forthcoming! The growing children all joined the Church
at ten, passing straight from Junior Sunday School into Church membership. At my first Communion I insisted that we rehearse the procedure on
the Saturday . . . the elders could give up their golf for once. I found they
had not even one goblet to consecrate . . . nothing but what reminded me of
the cruets with all the sauces you see in the Café Royal! I pled with them to
find some kind of suitable cup, and an elder named Campbell, who
pronounced his name 'Camel' rose to the occasion by going home and
bringing two lovely old Scottish pewter Communion Cups which he had
bought in an antique shop in the Royal Mile, not realising what they were . . .
they now use them regularly. The only wedding I had was a great social
occasion, in charge of a highly paid professional Directress of Ceremonies.
There were seven bridesmaids and seven groomsmen; she had them sized
off, exactly arranged in a flattened V facing the congregation, chalk marks
on the carpet where to stand, entry meticulously timed. At the ceremony
itself one couldn't see for flash bulbs of cameras taking close-ups. I believe
that marriage lasted a year.

It was the funerals that were most off-putting. The 'casket' would be
hinged in the middle so that the departed could be seen; the cortège was
preceded by two policemen on motor bikes with headlights on, and all
traffic had to go in to the side. Passing through the gateway to the cemetery
(owned by the 'mortician'); a beam was broken which signalled to the
musician playing the carillon on top of the hill, who broke into 'Shall we
gather at the river?' or something similiar; nothing so vulgar as earth was to
be seen . . . all was totally, decently covered with artificial grass. Instead of
throwing three handfuls of earth, I was given one perfect rosebud to lay on
the coffin. It seemed to me to be trying to sentimentalise away the grim
reality of death.

One was constrained to remark on differences such as these, and I was
asked to 'lay on' a Service as it would be in Cramond. We got Alex to tear
up one of the old Psalm Books with words and music divided and airmail
them over. I warned them they would have to come in time, and they did.
Colin put on a gown, and acted beadle, carrying in the Bible; a couple in the
Choir had a real wee baby christened . . . the baby cried but not too much.

We sang the Old Hundredth, French, Duke Street and Crimond, and the Choir sang St. George's, Edinburgh, as an anthem . . . it was great and they loved it. The same day the Wards had an identical Service in Cramond. As the end of our stay drew near the generosity of these kind people was overwhelming. The two main industries were peach farming and textiles. We would come in and find a bushel of fresh peaches at the front door and another at the back . . . we never made up on them and, of course, we couldn't take them home. Textiles we could and did. I was given eleven pairs of sheets and piles of towels of all sorts, face, bath, dish . . . the lot. We were even given ex-Army trunks to take them home . . . we arrived back with seventeen pieces of luggage. It was a great and unforgettable experience for us all.

Six years later, one of their members, Mrs Hanna, who owned and ran one of those wonderful Holiday Camps for girls, invited Catriona to come to her camp; she would be her guest from the moment she left Cramond Manse. So off she went, a twelve-year-old all on her own, seen off at Prestwick by the family. She sent a postcard from John Kennedy Airport: 'Arrived safely after a good flight. Met by a kind old gentleman from AAA (American Alcoholics Anonymous) who took me for a drink (a coke) and is seeing me on the plane for Spartanburg.' She was met on return, and came walking across the tarmac in high-heeled shoes, wearing a dress with the belt below her bottom, and chewing bubble gum . . . real young American? No fear. She described it to me:

'Dad, it was wonderful, we had everything, canoeing, water ski-ing, pony trekking – you name it. There were 300 girls, 298 Americans, a girl from Paris, and me . . . and I had to swear allegiance to the American flag every morning. Dad, it was horrible.'

Like the rest of us, she was charmed but not converted.

I have been back to the USA several times since then – to the Divinity College in Richmond, Virginia, and to Grace Covenant Church in that city, the Wards having moved there; to a Pastors' Conference at Columbus, Ohio, with 3,000 delegates; for eight miserable hot, noisy, crowded weeks in 5th Avenue Presbyterian Church, New York in 1960; to do Memorial Lectures in that City, and later in High Point, North Carolina; to the famous Summer Conference at Lake Chatauqua in its Centenary Year. Several times Jean and I have gone down again to Spartanburg and two wonderful friends there have taken us on holiday to Hilton Head, Daytona Beach and Fort Lauderdale. Belle Wardlaw's husband Jim was in charge of the pulpit arrangements on our exchange visit, and was kindness itself. After he died Belle teamed up with an old friend, Martha Andrews. She was an astonishing person, a widow, well left, for many years the champion clay-pigeon shot of America. They made a great pair. Belle was full of stories – one typical example was about the young man who bought a new horse for his surrey with the fringe on the top, and chose to call it 'Closer'. When he took his girl friend out for a drive he would shout to the horse: 'Giddup, Closer,' and the girl always did! These two personify and highlight our memories of friendship and kindness, as we think of the impressions of the States and the American people, from these many visits. I have always come back warmed by unfailing hospitality, stimulated by new ideas and other ways of doing things, but glad to be home, back where, in terms of my genes, I belong.

Having struck that note, and recalling the consideration which prompted my final, last-minute decision not to return to New Zealand, it may not come amiss if I describe briefly how the same issue arose in respect of America. I referred earlier to our eight weeks in 5th Avenue Presbyterian Church, New York, in 1960. I am afraid we found that great city coldly impersonal, unbearably noisy, and oppressively over-crowded. We missed the warm, friendly atmosphere of the South. After five of our eight weeks we went to the Massanetta Springs Conference in Virginia, where we had heard the strange prayers. Belle and Martha were there and, realising how difficult we were finding New York, took us home to the comparative peace and quiet of Spartanburg. I commuted by air the last three weekends, and it was worth it. After I had finished in 5th Avenue these two kind friends took us to a delightful motel at Daytona Beach. On our last day I got a long distance phone call from one of the trustees of 5th Avenue, saying the three of them wished to consult with me before I left on a matter of great importance. I pointed out that I had finished my contract with them and was on my way home. Under pressure I reluctantly agreed to go up with an earlier flight and meet them for lunch. Jean wisely pled another engagement and skived off.

They took me to the restaurant of the Four Caesars: incredibly expensive, but that was their style; they were big business tycoons, in the Rockefeller Institute, American Rubber and American Steel respectively. After lunch, having asked me how I liked New York, and how I liked their Church, and having received the most polite evasive answers I could muster up, they got down to business and explained that their Minister, Dr John Sutherland Bonnell (a Canadian) had indicated that he would be retiring in eighteen months' time. After these eight weeks there was a strong feeling among the office-bearers and, indeed, the Congregation, that they need look no further, but invite me to succeed him. What would I be doing in the meantime? I replied that I was returning to my own Congregation who had given me leave of absence. Would I give them an undertaking not to go anywhere else during these eighteen months? I replied:

'Gentlemen, you are treating this as a purely business proposition . . . you are trying to take out an option on my services for the next eighteen months; this is all highly improper.'

We parted not exactly on the best of terms; I think they were surprised and nonplussed . . . I was very angry. They were not put off; eighteen months later Dr Bonnell duly retired, and I received a formal invitation to become Minister of 5th Avenue . . . all spelled out: £10,000 stipend, which was about four times what anybody was getting then in Scotland, a flat in Park Lane, and three months' holiday a year, to be taken at my convenience, with all sorts of perks. I replied that I was too much of a Scot to transplant successfully in what I would find an alien situation; anyway, in view of America's position in world affairs, it was time they had a native American in that influential pulpit. I wrote two foolscap pages and got no acknowledgement. I don't think they understood how anyone could decline their handsome offer. No decision with far-reaching consequences ever worried me less.

No account of those twelve years in Cramond would be complete without some reference to the Romans who, after all, were there long before any of us. Indeed, one of the fringe benefits of living in Cramond was the unique way it ministered to my aforementioned sense of history. It had long been known that the Church and Manse were on the site of the Roman fort, and many important discoveries had been made over the years. This went on, with outstanding success, during our time. I mentioned earlier that during the building of the new Session House on the north side of the site of the fort, the modern builders had a lot of trouble with Roman walls well below the surface. Looking down into the excavation I said to the gaffer:

'These walls have lasted 1,700 years – will yours last as long?'

'Oh! no fear,' he replied, 'Far longer. They were pointing with mortar – we're doing it with cement.'

Be that as it may, it was very interesting when a party of archaeologists came and asked permission to 'do a dig' in the Manse garden – in fact it was in the hen-run! We had no hens 'in residence' at the time, and they could come out and shut the gate, safely leaving their dig open, and no one would fall into it. It was fascinating to watch. They dug a huge trench from east to west, hoping to cut the east wall of the fort, which they calculated from previous excavations ran north and south. They kept coming in with all sorts of finds: pottery, brooches etc., carrying us back as far as 300 AD. One day they came in to say they were going to finish and fill in – they couldn't understand why they hadn't found the wall of the fort. The very next day, great excitement. Could I come at once? They had dug another yard, and Eureka! – there, nine feet down in our hen-run was the cobbled Roman roadway and the retaining wall of the vallum. They dug another yard in either direction to establish the line. Then they got a geologist to come and use his probe, following the line and always getting clay from the in-fill. Having got out of the Manse garden into the market garden in what had been the glebe they lost the clay, cast around and found it again; following the new line they ended up in the schoolhouse garden, where there were many interesting finds at a comparatively shallow level. They now had two points from which to start; joining the lines produced they ended up at a point just north of the Church. They now realised that what had misled them was that the fort was not built 'square' NSEW, but 'diamond' and what they had come to was the northern apex. Having reached this conclusion they said: 'If the Romans built true, then the apex of the fort should be about here.' They dug down, and only eighteen inches below the surface – as against nine feet in our garden – was the corner of the fort, with the little shops built against the outside for good measure. It was one of the most important Roman finds in Scotland, further establishing that Cramond had been the main Roman port in that part of Scotland. To someone who had done Honours Classics and spent some weeks in the Forum at Rome, that was an unmistakable thrill.

Chapter 10

Convenerships

About this time, in the latter part of our period in Cramond, I began to become involved in the work of Assembly Committees. I have already explained how I sort of grew into being Convener of the Huts and Canteens Committee which, not falling under the five years' rule, whereby the Convener must retire after five years' service, meant that I remained in office for twelve years, which was very good experience. Then the scope of the Temperance Committee, having come to be regarded as too narrow and limiting, was widened to become the Committee on Temperance and Morals, and I was asked to take over. It was an important remit, involving as it did the increasing craze for gambling, fostered by the football pools, lotteries and, most insidious, the use of raffles, in one form or another, for raising money for all sorts of worthy causes. This led to understandable confusion. In the Village Hall one Saturday there would be a sale for the WRI – raffles galore, no holds barred. Next Saturday, with very much the same people involved, a similar sale under the auspices of the Woman's Guild, any form of raffles *verboten*, why the difference? We had to be ready to give positive reasons for the stance that we took. On the gambling through raffles issue, we tried to pose the question: 'How can you take money raised by appealing to people's covetousness – wanting something for nothing – under the heading of "Christian Liberality"?'

The same principle of being positive applied to the question of drinking alcohol. How could one justify the Committee's continuing recommendation that the most desirable practice for the Christian was total abstinence? We gathered together a team of famous sportsmen who willingly gave their testimony that this was their own personal practice for the sake of maximum fitness. It happened to be my own personal attitude – brought up that way, I was confirmed in it by a grim experience when I started playing football at University. On our first 'Meal Monday' tour to Leeds we were entertained on the evening after the match in the Liberal Club which lived up to its name. It ended up with myself, the only TT in the group, at the age of nineteen, taking the others home to the Hotel in penny numbers, in the wee sma' hoors. I took a scunner at the whole disgusting business. For years I was the bane of the existence of Edinburgh head waiters at wedding receptions by refusing to start the speechifying until orange juice was supplied for myself and at least the young people. I aligned myself alongside our team of sportsmen abstainers. In the light of the later escalation of problems like teenage drinking and alcoholism, I am quite prepared to refute the charge that the goalie was being too holy, even goody-goody. Having spoken about 'escalation of problems' it is worth recording that shortly after my Committee was merged with Social Service, and I became Joint Convener with Donald Davidson of the Social and Moral Welfare Board, we enquired of the Police and the Health authorities about the seriousness of the problems of drink and drugs. We got the reassuring reply that neither was large enough to merit our proposed special study – that would be about 1960.

That brings me to my move to the Convenership of the Stewardship and Budget Committee. The task of that Committee, still in its infancy, but rapidly growing in importance, was to persuade the Church, the whole Church, and not just the loyal members, who were already giving freely, often sacrificially, to think in terms of Christian Stewardship and Christian Liberality. Let's face it, there has been, and still is, much giving that is neither Christian nor liberal! Partly it is due to our mixed heritage. Members of the old UP and Free Churches, being entirely self-supporting, knew that they were dependent for their continued existence and effectiveness upon their own giving, so they were trained to give. Those from the old Parish Church tradition, however, so many of whose now inescapable responsibilities had fallen, by long tradition and even law, upon the heritors, the owners of land in the Parish, had never been trained to give – there was no need. I remember an old man telling me how, in his childhood: 'Father put a penny in the plate, and the whole family walked in!'

But that is not the whole of it. On my many visits to the USA it has always seemed to me that the average Church member budgets for the main priorities of living, food, clothing, housing, education and, in the same bracket, what they will give to the Church. Too many of our members tend to give out of the small change that is left when all the other needs are satisfied. It is very difficult to get people to think in terms of what we cheerfully and unthinkingly spend on ourselves. Take one example. Just before we went decimal I was asked to go and speak about Christian Stewardship in a Church on the west side of Glasgow. Just before we went into the pulpit the minister told me that the Congregation had just received their target for the Mission and Service Fund, it showed a considerable increase, and they were indignant – nothing like being assured of a hearty welcome! While he was conducting the first part of the Service I did some calculations. I got up and said:

'I believe you people are indignant at the increased target set you by the Presbytery for the Mission and Service Fund. You have every right to feel that way, for let me tell you what it means. For all the work of the Church outside your own parish, elsewhere in Scotland, and overseas, all the Social Service and caring activities, you are being asked to increase your giving from $3\frac{3}{4}d$. per head per week, to $6d$. It is iniquitous, it should not be allowed. But let me put two simple questions. I imagine that you men living in this area, support a certain famous football team, which I must not mention. By which turnstile will you get in for $6d$?'

The women all laughed. I turned to them:

'Ladies, you have laughed too soon. Where in this district will you get a shampoo and set for $6d$.? Tell me, and I'll bring a bus load of ladies from Edinburgh to take advantage of such a bargain.'

It at least made them think, which is something we often fail to do in this connection.

We are nearing the end in the stage of our story that covers those twelve years in Cramond, and a host of random memories clamour to be recorded. I seem to hear the ghost of Morag, our famous Shetland pony, whinnying to be remembered. She came from Shetland by boat and train when she was about the size of a golden retriever, and was walked to her destination in Barnton Avenue by a porter, who took her on a lead from Davidson's Mains station, she getting the lead round every lamp post on the way. Her owner had bought her for his grandchildren, who took no interest in her, so he offered her to me. I walked her down late on Christmas Eve and put her in the stable (like a true country parish manse we had stable, barn, granary – the lot). After the stockings had been emptied and presents opened on Christmas morning I told the family they had missed a present . . . frantic, fruitless search, till I dropped a hint: 'It's got a leg for each stocking.' Up went the shout: 'A pony!'

There was a small pneumatic-tyred cart and harness for her, with which they had great fun, and at garden fetes drives in the pony cart were a prize attraction. She was full of mischief. Hers was the centre stall in the stable with a bar across held in large staples. She soon discovered that by putting her head under one end and joogling it up and down the bar would fall down and she was away; coming in from visiting about 10.00 p.m. I would be sent to look for her. She would go next door into the great paddock at Cramond House – how do you find a dark brown pony in the black-out? She would stand quite still till you bumped into her or smelt her. If you missed her she would give a cheeky whinny: 'I've done you again!' On good Sundays she would stand at the little gate on the road down to the beach and receive offerings of pies, chips, apple cores etc.; she became quite a public figure, and even rated a reference in the *Daily Express*. When we were leaving for St. Cuthbert's a wonderful old lady, Mrs Pearson, who lived to 107, gave Morag a home on her small estate near Ratho. The old lady used to write me, as from Morag: 'Please don't worry about me – I am much better looked after here, by a kind old lady who gives me an apple every day, which is something you never did.' In that country setting we had all sorts of pets: white rabbits, a Belgian hare, guinea pigs, hamsters, white mice, bantams, even geese. We actually had a bantam hen who sat on a goose egg, falling off and getting on again until she hatched it out, getting a shock when the gosling came out.

The next memory that comes back to me is the sound of the Scouts, singing their jungle songs. We had many privileges in the Dalmeny Estate, camping in the laundry or the tattie workers' huts, and bridging the Cockle Burn. We also had several Easter camps at Mr Matthew Mather's sheep farm at Posso, in the Manor Valley. During one spell of bitter wind and rain I recall the shepherd exclaiming, with tears running down his cheeks: 'The lambs are dying as soon as they're born, and I can do nothing to save them.' Six boys from that Troop went into the Ministry. In a class by himself was Geoff Shaw who, after a spell in New York, tried to transplant the East Harlem experiment into Glasgow and founded and ran the Gorbals Group, living and working among the people he was trying to help. He went into local politics as a means of securing the changes so desperately needed; he progressed till he became the first Convener of Strathclyde Region, responsible for the welfare of half the people of Scotland, unashamedly continuing to use the Rev. before his name, respected, admired by people of all ranks and parties, and beloved by many. At 55 he killed himself by overwork, and I have never experienced anything like his funeral service in Glasgow Cathedral, where George MacLeod referred to him as 'a modern saint' – with that I cordially agree, and I am humbly grateful to have been associated with Geoff. The others were Gordon Simpson, later my Assistant in St. Cuthbert's, now Minister in Leslie; his cousin, Graeme Veitch, these many years a minister in New York State; Alasdair Elders, in Broughton

Macdonald Church; Terry Large, teacher of RE in a Fife School, and my own son Alan, one of HM Inspectorate for Community Education.

Another interest which began about that time, and was to have lasting effects, started when I allowed myself to be persuaded by Miss May Andrew, Headmistress of James Gillespie's High School for Girls, to become her School Chaplain. It was quite daft, me traipsing away from Cramond into town in time for Morning Assembly, but I enjoyed it thoroughly, and continued for twenty-five years. I was in a good succession, my predecessors in that office having been Prof. J.S. Stewart and the Rev. D.H.C. Read, who had become the first Chaplain to Edinburgh University, and was later to have a long and distinguished ministry in Madison Avenue, New York, from which, as I write, he has recently retired. Miss Andrew was a powerful personality who ran a school with high standards, both academically and in pride of belonging, which I fully shared. When she was retiring she told two stories against herself. One of the wee Primary girls went home and reported, instead of: 'Miss Andrew is retiring, and is having her portrait painted' – 'Miss Andrew is so tired she's having to have her face painted!' Another time she was walking over Bruntsfield Links in front of the old School, with another of the wee ones hopping and skipping around her, when the child suddenly said: 'Miss Andrew, do you know why it is I'm so clever?'

'No, dear.'

'It's because I was at another school before I came to Gillespie's!'

I continued in the post under Miss Steel and Miss McIvor. I happened to be Moderator the year the new School was opened by the Queen Mother, so I had the pleasure of being associated with Her Majesty when I did the Dedication. The School presented me with an extra set of Moderatorial lace. Last November, when I was acting as locum in Fairmilehead Parish Church, we were having a Uniformed Organisations Parade. When we met to rehearse the Colour Party ceremonial the Guide Captain said: 'I helped to pay for your lace!' I keep coming across old girls all over the world – their affection for their old Chaplain is very heartwarming. My most poignant memory of those twenty-five years goes back twenty years to the first Assembly of the New Year. Before Christmas, one of the senior girls, Elaine Anderson, one of those who are good at everything, had played the lead in the School pantomime, happy, full of life. During the holidays her father had taken a brainstorm and killed Elaine, her twelve-year-old brother and her grandmother and seriously injured her mother. Can you imagine the feelings of some six hundred schoolgirls, faced with that hideous tragedy? What could one say? Taking that Assembly was one of the hardest things I ever had to do.

Tragedies like that, baffling both mind and heart, and making one cry, as did Christ on the Cross: 'My God, why?' were balanced by deliverances just as mysterious, indeed miraculous. At the height of the polio epidemic I was phoned at 10 o'clock one Sunday morning by a tearful father, telling me that his ten-year-old son John was gravely stricken, and was not expected to live out the day – would I ask the congregation to pray for him? I explained the situation and we all prayed, specifically and fervently for John. The Cargilfield School pupils prayed for him each night in their dorm, and the Cubs, with whom he belonged, prayed for him at their meeting. I visited him regularly in his iron lung in the Royal Infirmary, the lung taking over his breathing from his useless muscles. I went in specially on Christmas Day, and found the small boy's head, sticking out of the iron lung, crowned with a cowboy hat. I asked Sister what was happening, and she replied: 'I'll pull him out for a minute and let you see the lot.' There he was, his helpless limbs fully dressed in cowboy chaps, with the regulation frilled top; in each hand was a 6-shooter; up they came, pointed at my chest with the demand: 'Stick 'em up!' John didn't die; he is still alive with only a minor disability in one foot – a happier story that still raises the question: 'Why? Why does one child, prayed for, recover, and another, equally prayed for, die?'

There is one further area of involvement, important and widely influential, which should be mentioned, developed in the Cramond years and carried forward to St. Cuthbert's, namely radio and later television. The Christmas after we came back from Dunedin the BBC asked me to do a special overseas broadcast for Scots overseas; to make it personal I was to send greetings by name to representative Scots around the world. I sent to Alex, the beadle's son, a Hudson Bay fur trader; my Suez Canal pilot; a couple doing forestry in Nigeria; a missionary in India; a young man jackarooing in Queensland; and a sheep farmer in New Zealand – and none of them – but none . . . got the message! Another time, on a hot August morning we did an Overseas Broadcast, which was being recorded and sent out later to different parts of the world. We had a blind organist, Frank Morrison whose guide dog usually lay quite unnoticed beside the organ pedals. For this occasion Frank thought it safer to leave him outside, so he chained him just below the window behind the organ. We began by singing 'The Lord of heaven confess', one of the great Psalms of praise. From outside, the dog joined in, and kept it up through all five verses! Twice later in the day we listened to the Service, and the dog sang round the world. We had one of the earliest TV Services which achieved a high rating, the country setting having its special appeal. The cameras often centred on one of the Cargilfield small boys who looked angelic with his fair hair and blue eyes – the Headmaster told me later he was probably the biggest rascal in the School. Shortly before we left Cramond I did a series of radio programmes, later published in pamphlet form, based on the carving in St. Cuthbert's Church of da Vinci's painting of The Last Supper, little dreaming that in a few months I would be standing under that carving hundreds of times in the following nineteen years. To that dramatic upheaval we must now turn.

Chapter 11

St. Cuthbert's

I don't suppose anyone, least of all the good folk of St. Cuthbert's at the time, ever realised what a traumatic experience it was for me – and my family – to leave Cramond and go to St. Cuthbert's. To leave Cramond at all for anywhere else was very hard. We had enjoyed, and were still enjoying to the full, these twelve years in what was really a country setting, where there was a warm community feeling; the youngsters did everything together, even to going down *en masse* to the cinema in South Queensferry on a Saturday evening; it was a growth area, with more and more young couples with families moving in and making the life and activities of the Church part of their lives . . . there was every encouragement. It would have been far easier, happier, and, yes, more sensible, to stay and live out one's ministry, usefully, rewardingly, and not unsatisfyingly. We were being asked to go to a central City Church, where 'the tide was going out', people were moving away; the trend for young people getting married and rearing their families was to move to the suburbs, even to come to Cramond! St. Cuthbert's itself could not have been more foreign to my traditions, heritage and upbringing. My background was plainness to the point of ugliness in Church building and decor – there was the strange idea that treacly black varnish over all woodwork was somehow peculiarly sacred; our Church in Kilmarnock did not have a proper Communion Table, only a peculiar affair with long legs, which was pulled forward and placed over the organ console on Communion Sundays.

We even exported this attitude; in First Church, Otago, in Dunedin, where Burns' nephew was minister, there was no Communion Table at all. As often happens the Kirk had come to be known by the name of its most truly 'ruling' elder, and it was known as 'Adams' Kirk'. Early this century some congenital idiot on the Kirk Session proposed that they instal a Communion Table. Adams reacted typically and violently: 'Over my dead body,' so they dropped the heretical proposal. A few years later Adams duly died, and they put in a Communion Table as a Memorial to him, which was as near over his dead body as they could get. But that was the kind of atmosphere and ethos. There was what was almost a cult of this plainness in worship, with a prejudice against read prayers, even more, prayers out of a book. The dignified ceremonial and processing in liturgy and worship were strange to me, and I don't think I had ever in my life led a congregation in reciting the Apostles' Creed (though I had preached my way through it in Dunedin). The whole ethos, the great traditions, the status of a great City Church like St. Cuthbert's I had never known. Cramond had been an old Parish Church, but a reasonably small country Parish Church; the very vastness of the building, after the 'couthiness' of Cramond, with the four galleries and the people all gathered round, overwhelmed me. I had done the Holy Week Services in St. Cuthbert's the previous year. On Good Friday evening I went in very early and sat in the back seat of the gallery just to meditate. I thought: 'You would need binoculars to see the detail of the carving above the Table.' I remember Jean and myself walking on the Braid Hills on a blustery March day, trying to find two arguments that the good Lord would accept, why we should not leave Cramond. It became one more of those inescapable things which we had to do.

Once the decision was taken a new problem arose – there was no Manse. For long enough St. Cuthbert's had gone on the principle that it is wrong to saddle a man with the house that suited his predecessor – you might change from a man with a large family to a bachelor, or vice versa – and, remember, they always had the two collegiate ministers to house. So, no Manse; instead, a Manse Allowance, which had not been updated for some time. Fortunately the Session got a timely legacy, which enabled them to buy (for £5,300 in 1956) a fine house in Wester Coates Road, just beyond Donaldson's Hospital, and just over a mile from the Church. There we were to spend nineteen happy years, and the family completed the process of growing up. Nor was there any doubting the warmth of the Congregation's welcome to this 'cuckoo in the nest'; 777 people crowded into the Upper Hall for the welcome Social, at which Dr Charles Warr of St. Giles' delivered himself of the interesting statement that: 'It is as near certain as can be that there was a Church of some sort where St. Cuthbert's now is, at least 250 years before there was any Church where St. Giles' now is.'

However long the history we were now entering an era of transition, and violent at that. I had gone to succeed Dr Adam Burnet as Junior Colleague to Dr White Anderson in the Collegiate Charge. It was the policy of '121' to get rid of such charges whenever opportunity occurred. On investigating the

St. Cuthbert's against the Castle

situation in St. Cuthbert's they discovered that it was unique. All the other Collegiate Charges in Scotland were First and Second Charges, with a clear distinction of status; St. Cuthbert's always had two ministers of absolutely equal status (at one time there were three!). The only distinction was that the one who had been inducted first to St. Cuthbert's was Senior. It took a lot of heated debate, a special Congregational Meeting, and a special Act of the General Assembly to make me, for the duration of my tenure of office, sole Minister of St. Cuthbert's (for the first time since the Reformation), to be supported by 'a Minister of The Church of Scotland, with experience'! Many members, quite naturally, resisted and resented what they saw as a lowering of the status of their beloved Church.

The status of the Associate took some working out, to avoid down-grading him to a glorified Assistant on the one hand, or bringing back the Collegiate system in a disguised form on the other. Was he appointed and installed by the Kirk Session, or did the Congregation in some sense 'call' him; did the Presbytery hold a Service of Admission and grant him a seat in the Presbytery? While all this ecclesiastical politicising was going on, I was having, still new, raw, and awkward, to try to run this huge Congregation. Dr Anderson took ill the very day I preached as Sole Nominee, never really functioned, and died suddenly in December of that same year, 1956. I would never have managed without the support of Dr David Steel, with his ability and experience, who acted as interim Associate for eighteen months, between coming home from Kenya and going to St. Michael's, Linlithgow. Once the system got going it worked well, though it was always a testing relationship for all our variously gifted Associates, Alwyn Macfarlane, David Hamilton, David Reid, and Ian Wotherspoon – we had all been accustomed to 'running our own show'!

As to the 'show' I was trying to run, having been, as indicated above, Sole Minister *de facto* if not *de jure* from the day I was inducted, there were decisions I had to make, responsibilities I had to take upon myself. The first was to change the arrangements for celebrating the Sacrament of Baptism. I was staggered to find that Baptisms were not held in the Service at all! The choir processed out, the congregation skailed; after an interval the choir processed in again singing a Baptismal Hymn, followed by any families with babies who happened to have turned up. There was no preparation, no instruction, no one knew who was coming. I was on safe ground with that immediate change, for I could appeal to my old friend, John Knox: 'Baptism shall be in face of the congregation' – not behind their backs after they have gone home!

Another decision was to set up a scheme to clean and redecorate the Church, and instal a new and more efficient public address system – I found that the stained glass windows (and they were all stained glass) had not been washed since George MacLeod's time. The long-term ambitious project of building the great new organ, with the main organ in the North Gallery and the console on the south side of the apse, had just been completed, and this seemed to demand a brighter and better setting. In carrying out this scheme we were advised by Ian Lindsay, the well-known Church architect, who imaginatively took the blue-green colour from the ceiling over the apse and put it throughout the Church. It was only after he died that his widow told me he was colour blind – she advised him on colours. For this project the Congregation generously raised a large sum of money, with enough left over to redecorate the Halls also. The net result was a much brighter and more beautiful place of worship – a far cry from my hereditary dark varnish! I set about trying to visit systematically round this huge and scattered congregation – an almost impossible task; I was also deliberately doing most of the baptisms, marriages, funerals, hospital visits etc., all of which created

Interior of St. Cuthbert's Church

personal relationships and broke down the mass. I acclimatised happily to the liturgy and ceremonial, and came to cherish the dignity and solemnity of the Communion Service. My sense of history was ministered to as never before, as I studied the Charter of King David I, giving the land round the Castle Rock of Edinburgh to St. Cuthbert's, dated 1127 and the oldest document in Scotland; or dipped into the huge tome *The Relics of St. Cuthbert*, sent us by Durham Cathedral; or looked at the very 'kenspeckle' pectoral cross, with its background of red shell from the shores of the Indian Ocean, dated by the British Museum as from the end of the seventh century, or the tablet of very ancient oak, roughly 7″ by 9″, reputed to be a portable altar carried by Cuthbert on his missionary journeys, and dated by X-rays in the same period; or handled the four original communion cups purchased in 1619, and costing more than the combined stipends of the two Ministers!

Yet from all this exciting heritage one kept being forced back into the harsh realism of the contemporary stage of drastic change and transition. This great Congregation had long carried out its work and witness, inspired and motivated by its worship, through various activities focused on the two Missions, in Freer Street and Morrison Street, in crowded areas of very poor housing. Now the people were moving away, the houses were coming down (between two Communions an Elder's district physically disappeared). Freer Street was just waiting to be finally closed down and cleared out, and a few years later Morrison Street, too, came to an end. St. Cuthbert's had lost a worthwhile, necessary and valuable function . . . and what was to take its place?

We carried out over the years three Parish Visitations, going to every home, and realising the lack of people, especially the young. Within the Congregation we had a major, carefully-planned Christian Stewardship Campaign centring around a meal at which 1,600 sat down in a huge marquee in the grounds of Donaldson's Hospital . . . out of that we got several keen new elders and greatly increased liberality and the mobilisation of many forms of service. We also got rid of seat rents as so many people were asking; 'If we are to think in terms of Christian Stewardship, why pay for a seat in God's house, as in the cinema or theatre?'

One of the happiest features of those early days was the development of closer relationships with our neighbours in St. John's Scottish Episcopal Church. This has gone on over the years and recently arrived at an ecumenical linking, with full approval from the top level authorities. We began with joint Holy Week Services, held in each Church alternately; experimented with joint Baptisms on Maundy Thursday, having found two babies of 'mixed parentage' (one of them my own granddaughter Fiona); even a joint Confirmation. In a series of Lenten studies 'Ways of celebrating Communion', we did a post-Reformation Communion, and this became a regular feature, serving fifty at a time, seated around trestle tables spread before the front pews. At one such Service the Bishop of Edinburgh was a Con-Celebrant. It is interesting that in the Order which we were following, it was laid down that 'during the serving of Communion, Scripture passages shall be read, relating to the Passion of our Lord, to divert the attention of the participants from the elements themselves to that which they signify.' We ourselves derived from this practice the custom of serving in that fashion at the early Communion on Easter Day. I have since done it, with much acceptance, in a Church in Melbourne and in the London Scottish Chapel of St. Columba's Church in London.

Chapter 12

Australia

The mention of Melbourne brings me naturally to the next special occasion . . . indeed the first of many. In 1962 the Rev. Gordon Powell, Minister of St. Stephen's Presbyterian Church, Sydney, invited me to go out for three months as guest preacher to his Church. We flew out this time, sending in advance by ship a trunk with our heavier clothing. We travelled in a Comet – a lovely aircraft – touching down at Rome, Beirut, and Karachi, before landing at Calcutta, where we were met by Peter Logan Ayre, who had been one of my successors in Bathgate. My main impression driving in from the airport at Dum-dum was of dirt, disease and death – that, along with the oppressive heat, still stays with me. Peter took us to the Scots Kirk; it is in the same square as the notorious Black Hole, also the Anglican Cathedral. The two buildings were going up at the same time; the bishop was insisting that his building must be higher – in the architectural sense – but the Scot out-did him, for his Kirk has a weather cock on top and is 18″ higher. Any taxi driver in Calcutta would drive you unhesitatingly to 'The Cock Church'!

We also visited a Mission School with a Scots missionary and four Indian teachers, beautifully dressed for the occasion. They had 160 children; they sat cross-legged on the tramped earth floor – total equipment a slate and slate pencil for each pupil, blackboard and chalk for teacher. Peter also showed me a striking contrast. He advised Jean not to come when he took me to a Hindu temple, its courtyard full of sick, diseased, with hideous disfigurements. In the centre of the yard was fixed a Y-shaped stick; each morning they put the head of a goat in it, cut its throat and let the blood run down – this was supposed to heal these hopeless people. He then took me to a simple building, just round the corner, with tiled walls and floor and straw on the floor . . . plain but redolent of love and caring. It was a 'Centre for the destitute Dying', run by a nun called Mother Teresa. Next day we flew

on to Rangoon, Singapore, Djakarta, and landed at Darwin at 2.00 a.m.
where we had to go through customs and immigration. I should have
mentioned that there was an outbreak of cholera in Calcutta (the Australian
government sent a plane-load of anti-cholera vaccine – they had to send a
squad of soldiers to guard it safely to the hospitals as even these life-saving
drugs would have been stolen and sold in the black market). We had our
documents checked by a bearded doctor, exactly like James Robertson
Justice, who made us stand aside, then said: 'I've got to vaccinate you two;
I'm not bothered about cholera, but your vaccination certificates are not in
order; they've got your GP's signature all right, but you didn't take them to
the Health Office to be rubber-stamped.'

When we eventually arrived in Sydney, by contrast to that rather 'sticky'
reception, there could be no doubt of the warmth of our welcome. The
Minister of St. Stephen's, Rev. Gordon Powell, had a flair for publicity, and
he had arranged for us to be received with all possible honours! The Prime
Minister, Bob Menzies, came and read the Lesson, and welcomed us on
behalf of the people of Australia (the next time we went Australia House
lost our passports). That wonderful little lady, his wife, Dame Patty,
thanked Jean for her singing beside her in the pew. When Bob came to

Outside St. Stephen's Church, Sydney, with Bob Menzies, Dame Patty, and Jean

Edinburgh eighteen months later, to be installed as the first Australian Knight of the Thistle, he kindly sent us tickets for the Service in St. Giles', and the reception in Holyrood. When we entered the drawing room in the Palace, the new Knight of the Thistle came striding across and, shaking hands, declared, 'My heart and my flesh crieth out for the living God,' which had been the text at that Service in 1962. In 1971, when I visited him in Melbourne, after he had a stroke and was physically handicapped but mentally clear as a bell, he told me a lovely story about that visit to Edinburgh. On his way home five hundred Australians gave him a lunch in London, at which he said: 'During the Installation Service I listened carefully to what Lord Lyon said, for what Lyon says, goes, this side of eternity. He repeatedly referred to me as "Sir Robert Meengies", so you must now correct your habitual mispronunciation of my guid Scots name. But you had better be consistent, for I have a fellow Knight who also pronounces his name oddly by our standards. So, in future, you will sing a famous song: "Hume, sweet Hume".' I have always regarded Sir Robert as the last of the Empire Statesmen . . . since him we have had nothing but politicians.

To begin with we stayed in a rather second-rate boarding house, just north of the bridge, at a place called Kirribilli, the point being that rather poorly paid office workers could stay there and cross cheaply on the ferry to their work in the city. We had two rooms inter-connecting; I suppose one was intended to be my study. Neither had any form of heating and the winter in Sydney was not quite over and was still cold. Our hostess, the minister's wife, brought us an old-fashioned paraffin stove, which we christened, for obvious reasons, 'Smelly Nelly'! Imagine us sitting crouched over Smelly Nelly, each wrapped in a blanket, with one hand outside to turn the leaves of our book, changing hands when that one got too cold. Fortunately we were given stone 'pigs' so that we managed to get warm enough to sleep. The arrangement for meals was unusual. There was a good, full dinner, waitress served, in the evening with all the residents back from work. Breakfast was somewhat off-putting; you went into the kitchen which was presided over by a fat Swedish cook, loosely held together by the strings of her greasy apron. She greeted me; 'Fawt you want for breakfast?' 'Can I have bacon and egg, please?' She took a plate off the rack over the range, slapped onto it a fried egg and rashers of bacon, wiped the edge of the plate with her apron and handed it over. Jean stuck to cornflakes and nothing else. On a good morning we would escape to a sheltered nook by the harbour, where Jean worked on her tapestry of da Vinci's 'The Last Supper', and I read aloud to her. One morning I spotted a cargo ship coming in to dock, and realised it was from Glasgow, carrying our trunk. Believe it or not, it cost more to get the trunk through customs and deliver it across the bridge, than to bring it all the way from Glasgow!

After about three weeks Jean took a bad sore throat, not surprisingly, and a friend came in his capacity as a doctor. This opens up an area of very special happy and lasting relationships. The Doctor was Albert Himmelhoch. He and his wife Jean both belonged to Sydney, and had met without paying much attention to each other. They met again in Edinburgh and, whether mutual homesickness had anything to do with it or not, they reached the point of wanting to get married. I had in Cramond, as my Assistant, a young minister from Sydney, Ross Flockhart, who knew them from Sydney, so I married them in Cramond in October, 1954. When Albert discovered the conditions in which Jean and I were living he promptly abducted us and took us to stay with them in their delightful home in the pleasant suburb of Killara on the North Shore. To look ahead a bit, I have stayed with them on all subsequent visits to Australia and have now married all four of their children, and christened six of their grandchildren.

Perhaps it was the opening publicity, but very soon we were having overflows at both Morning and Evening Services, as many as two hundred in the Hall – the number always announced by Gordon, because during the first singing the beadle held up a large numbered card in the back of the Gallery! But what was 'out of this world' was an amazing Lunch Hour Service on a Wednesday from 1.15 to 1.45 p.m., absolutely packed out – people from the huge office blocks and stores, many young, brought their sandwiches and thermos flasks, and ate their lunch in the pew during the talk. There was one mad week when Catherine Marshall, widow of Peter Marshall, 'A Man called Peter', was there to boost the sales of her new book 'To live again' – they were in every corner, in brush cupboards and passage ways, with about two hundred out on the pavement in the rain. We shared the Service – she took seventeen minutes and left me three for my course of talks. All this was thrilling and exciting, but it left us little time to get about and see the country.

One of the elders, Alan Evans, kindly took us down the South Coast as far as Kiama, where there is a spouting cave, not nearly as spectacular as Iona! Another time he took us to visit Canberra – this was before they had the lake, and it had no appearance or character. We met the Minister for Social Services, one of the sons of Sir Hugh Roberton, the famous conductor of the Glasgow Orpheus Choir. He gave us dinner in the members' dining-room, and got us into the House to view a session. It was so cold I had to wear my pyjama trousers as long johns under my trousers.

It was the second coldest day ever recorded in the Capital! On the way home next day, towards dusk we took a fatal short-cut which brought us down a narrow road, with no chance of turning, to a ford over a fairly full-running river. We decided to chance it, and stuck mid-stream, with the water above the door-sills. Alan and I had to take off shoes and stockings, and get out and shove, well over knee deep. Jean leaned forward from the back seat and tried to steer; in the process she sounded the horn, and I shouted: 'Look out! Alan, we're being overtaken.' That helped us to make a joke of what might have been a nasty situation; mercifully the engine started, and we drove to an old inn with a huge log fire at which we dried ourselves.

A specially pleasant trip we did more than once was when Jean and Albert took us to their holiday home at Blackheath in the Blue Mountains. The drive up is fantastic; you wend your way among these tumbled ridges and deep valleys, with the great trees which give off the blue haze which gives the mountains their name, and you can understand how they posed an impenetrable barrier to the fertile lands beyond. The first road, built mainly with convict labour, was an engineering marvel, and its modernised form gives access to a string of resorts of great scenic beauty. The air is clear and invigorating, and can be cold, for Blackheath is 2,000' high. On one occasion we went even further to the lovely pastures around Orange, and all the great spread of farming wealth that was there, waiting to be claimed, 'beyond the ranges'.

Quite early on we had a special expedition to Brisbane for the Centenary of St. Andrew's Church, where Hugh and Isobel Douglas had been on a similar remit to ours. We had a great concert in the City Hall, with the Lord Mayor in the chair. We had everything, orchestras, choirs, soloists, vocal and instrumental, elocutionists – the lot. I got on at 10.15 p.m. to make the main speech. I told the story of Jock Howieson and the King at Cramond Brig – the story enshrined on the War Memorial in Cramond Kirk. King James V was accustomed to going about in the guise of an ordinary citizen, the guid man o' Ballengeich. He was crossing Cramond Brig when he was set upon by a group of gipsies, who saw only a well-dressed traveller worth beating up. A farm labourer, Jock Howieson, was threshing corn with an old-fashioned flail near his cottage by the brig. Hearing the noise he dashed in, laid about him with his flail, drove off the gipsies, and in all probability saved the King's life. Without any idea of the identity of the man he had rescued, Jock took him to his cottage and cleaned and bound up his wounds. The King, duly grateful, asked what he could do in return for this signal service. Jock replied: 'Well, like any true Scot I would like to own a bit of Scotland, but there's no chance – all the land about here belongs to the King.' The King explained that he had some influence at court, and might be able to arrange for Jock to meet the King and see if something might be done. 'And mind, Jock,' he said, 'You'll be able to recognise him, because he'll be the only man with his bonnet on.' So Jock duly went to Holyrood and met his friend, wondering why so many were so respectful. Then he asked: 'What about meeting the King?' to which the monarch replied: 'You remember I told you he would be the only man with his bonnet on.' 'Well,' says Jock, 'it must be you or me, we're the only twa wi' our bonnets on!' The King revealed his identity, and gifted the lands around Cramond Brig to Jock and his heirs in perpetuity, on one interesting condition – that if a descendant of the King crossed Cramond Brig, a descendant of Jock would bring water and wash the hands of the King's descendant. When our present Queen first stayed at Holyrood after her accession, Houieson Craufurd of Craufurdland Castle took a silver basin and ewer and a linen towel, poured water over the Queen's hands and renewed his right to the lands.

I quoted this delightful story as an example of what we Scots should do to keep alive our traditions. At the end a woman came up to me with the tears running down her face and said: 'You'll never believe it, but my husband is a distant descendant of Jock Howieson, and the house we live in here in Brisbane is called "Cramond Brig".' I then asked the Lord Mayor if it would be difficult to find out how many of those who took part in the concert had some Scots connections. He replied that it would be easy, as they were all having a party, and he would go and see. He came back and said: 'Every human being who was on the platform, including myself, was either born in Scotland or comes of Scottish stock.'

To return briefly to the main object of our visit to Sydney, the phenomenon of the large attendances continued to the end. At their August communion there were 1,450 people took part, which they told me was a record. When it came to leaving we had a great send off as we boarded the *Arcadia* to sail home. We called in at Fremantle, and paid our first visit to the lovely city of Perth (apart from passing through in 1950), where we stayed with the parents-in-law of Alwyn Macfarlane, my associate. I also was requested to visit the Presbyterian Church of Western Australia, which had a Moderator and a General Assembly, the whole set up. I was staggered to find that the total membership was smaller than that of St. Cuthbert's. We then had a long stretch across the Indian Ocean to Colombo, where the Minister was now Andrew Baillie, supported by his sister Martha. The houseservant, who was a Buddhist, had made a beautiful flower arrangement in the form of a Cross, in honour of the 'Big Jesus Man'. We met with the various organisations of the Church and realised how important for exiles of all sorts outposts of the Kirk like this continue to be.

The long trip from Colombo to Bombay, with the hot air coming off the coast of India, was enlivened by two events. They carried out a 'Man Overboard' exercise. When we were steaming at full speed, a lifebuoy with a marker was thrown overboard, and the alarm whistles sounded. Without immediately reducing speed the huge ship was turned in a wide circle, bringing her almost back to where the buoy had been dropped; the launch was lowered, her propellor turning almost before she hit the water, and the buoy was picked up – time from sounding the alarm 12 minutes, back to the ship 18. Considering the speeding weight of such a ship and, of course, no brakes, it was very reassuring. Later the same day we were shown over the galley. I found the facts and figures so striking that I make no apology for quoting them – just as an example of what we take for granted in the daily provision for our deeper needs. On that ship, the *Arcadia*, there were 130 table stewards and 70 on the chef's table; 6,000 meals were served daily to passengers and crew. On a voyage of 9 weeks (during which we had hopped on) 165,000 eggs and 70,000 pints of milk would be used. I felt like quoting: 'He satisfieth thy mouth with good things'! The end of that particularly hot stretch brought us to Bombay, already visited in 1950 on the way to New Zealand.

Bombay had changed . . . there was not so much of the dreadful refugee problem; Mr Beck, the minister, told us that his congregation numbered about 150, with eleven elders, four of them Indians, and the character of the congregation was changing, with more younger men, mainly technicians coming out on special jobs for, say, two years. We enjoyed a lot of hospitality and met many friends. We had to leave without tugs because of a strike, but managed it by careful seamanship. The next port of call was Aden once again; this time we went ashore and visited the Church of Scotland hospital at Sheikh Othman where one of our Cramond boys, Harry Robertson, was a doctor. I shall never forget the sight, in their hospital, of two figures in cots next to each other. In one, a laughing, happy three-year-old, full of life; in the other, lying listlessly, what looked like a wizened old woman, in fact another child of the same age, just brought in suffering from extreme malnutrition. The staff were very thrilled because the Boys' Brigade of Scotland had made the hospital their special scheme for that year and had raised enough money to air-condition the operating theatre, so that the surgeon operating did not find the perspiration running down his hands into the wound. How much we take for granted.

After leaving Aden we decided to take in the special tour to Cairo and the

Pyramids. As we got into the Gulf of Suez, in spite of the blazing heat we had a clear view, to starboard, of the Sinai massif, with all its associations – it all looked terribly desolate and forbidding. Landing at Suez in the very early morning, we were driven by special bus 97 miles by way of Heliopolis, now a huge Egyptian army camp, to Cairo. We managed to rise to morning coffee in the famous Shepheard's Hotel. We then visited the Museum, particularly fascinated by all the objects from Tutankhamen's tomb, from the gilded chair, the three gold coffins and four gilded shrines, to the seeds of corn, wheat etc. for the dead man to sow in the after-life. The curator had tried sowing some of these ancient seeds and they grew! From there to the gorgeous Mosque of Mohammed Ali, then the Pyramids and the Sphinx – she is getting a bit weathered. Crawling up and down inside the Great Pyramid was back-breaking and claustrophobic, but it did something special for my sense of history. Built in 2,900 BC, 450' high and the same square – how on earth was it done? After all the sightseeing we were faced with a long drive, through villages that depressed one with their appalling poverty, finally to Port Said and the ship. It was an experience I would not have missed. The final, uneventful stage through the Mediterranean brought us to Barcelona, of which I remember almost nothing; we were unable to do any sightseeing for the torrential rain. From there, we flew home.

Nine years passed – very eventful years for us both. Jean had started her Parkinson's Disease and undergone her brain operation; I had been Moderator, among other things. Australia came on the agenda again. Gordon Powell had moved to Scots Church, Melbourne, where there is a famous arrangement, known as the Turnbull Trust Preaching Lectureship. The background is that at the turn of the century a farmer's son from Eyemouth, having lost an arm, was more or less dumped as useless, and went off to Australia. By a combination of hard work and good fortune he became a very wealthy man, and set up the large Turnbull Trust, half the income to be used for the upkeep of Scots Church, of which he was very fond; the other half to bring out a guest preacher, preferably from Scotland, for three months every third year, when the interest had accrued. This was as a Memorial to his sons killed in World War I. This began in 1926 and has continued; after World War II, in which there were further family casualties, the rest of the family added to the original Trust, so that the scheme might continue, in spite of rising costs.

The names of those who have been Turnbull Trust Preacher reads like a kind of Hall of Fame, and it was an honour to be asked, as Gordon then asked me to be the preacher for 1971. By getting an extension of the normal summer holiday period to leave of absence it became possible. We decided,

List of Turnbull Trust Preachers (Note RLS three times)

in view of the new problem of Jean's health, to take a stop-over in Athens and Hong Kong. We had four days in Athens, kindly and skilfully looked after by Bill Tudhope, brother-in-law of John Ellis, my Deputy Session Clerk, whose local knowledge was invaluable. In addition to doing the sights of Athens itself, marvelling at the glory of the Parthenon, and following in the footsteps of St. Paul to the agora and Mars Hill, with the added delight of a 'son et lumière' programme, we did a conducted tour of the south of Greece, going first to Corinth. We saw the value of the Corinth canal, cutting across the Isthmus, and avoiding the dangerous seas around Cape Matapan (where Prince Philip fought as a young naval officer). In the early days they used to put their small ships on rollers, and pull them across

– exactly like the several Tarberts in the west of Scotland, 'tarbet' or 'tarbert' meaning 'a place for pulling boats across'. In Corinth itself we saw all the excavated area, and what is still going on; then on to Mycenae, with its famous Lion Gate and vast circular tombs, dating to about 1500 BC; the Tomb of Agamemnon, a vast beehive building 60′ high – the stone lintel, all one piece, weighs 120 tons – again, how did they do it? What impressed us most was Epidaurus with its theatre dating from the 1st century BC. In its semi-circular tiers of seats it can accommodate 15,000; Maria Callas sang to 17,000. The acoustics are incredible, for there is no 'backcloth' of any kind, just the open flat stage. Two small children said a recitation on the sand-floored stage, and every word could be heard in the back row! We need microphones to be audible in a big room.

At the end of that delightful interlude, which catered for the Greek half of my classical upbringing, we flew on to Hong Kong, to stay with Jean's nephew, Kenneth Finlayson and his wife, Margaret. Ken was the manager of a big Insurance firm; they stayed in a beautiful flat on the Peak. They showed us round in a big way, driving us all over the Island and into the New Territories, looking over into Red China, and passing Sek Kong where our Church of Scotland Hut used to be (now pulled down, and replaced by housing). I was very impressed by the huge reservoir created by shutting off a deep bay with an island in the middle with walls across to the shore on either side; fresh water previously had had to be brought from China . . . and paid for. On the Sunday they took us for a boat picnic, which was lovely. They jointly own it with another Scot, Willie Purves, who had a son at Cargilfield; they bought it second hand for £750. We were taken to the moorings in a sampan steered by an elderly Chinese woman, and went to a large island called Lamma, where we anchored for the day. We had a speedboat in tow, so the girls, Clare, twelve, and Jill, ten, practised water-skiing; even I swam. When we got home after a great day, we were ferried this time by an attractive young Chinese mother, with a baby asleep in the stern, and two older boys, probably six and five working the ropes.

Another outstanding boat trip was arranged by Alex Maclennan, one of my elders, to the island of Hay Ling Chau. It was a colony for sufferers from leprosy, founded by a Scot, Dr Neil Fraser. It originally housed five hundred, mostly from mainland China; the numbers had fallen, because of improved control of the disease. It was a wonderful place. The Superintendent explained that the reason some of the patients were off-putting to look at was because of injuries sustained through loss of sensation. They can do wonders through surgery; plastis to the face, giving muscle control, or the power to close the eyes, so that the patient can sleep again! They can take a muscle from the wrist, divide it into four, and give back the use of the fingers and the hand. We saw over the hospital and met the surgeon, Dr Grace Warren from Sydney, who does these wonderful operations. We also visited 'the Lord is willing' Church, for the 92 members, very light and cool. The pews were supplied by children in Scotland, who gave to the Leprosy Mission. They raised more than was needed so the pews are made of teak. I believe it is all now closed down, but it was a wonderful experience of skilled, compassionate, constructive Christian caring.

The Finlayson family also took us to all sorts of 'posh' eating-places, like the prestigious Fan Ling Golf Club, of which I am an honorary life member, by virtue of having flown over it in a helicopter! Our few happy days in Hong Kong were ended. Jean had never felt at ease there – too many people crowded into too small a space; having been there before, I must confess I always found its life, even its political existence, to be artificial. Flying south to Australia we landed at Sydney, where we were met in transit by Graham and Hazel Hardy – Graham had gone out from Palmerston Place Church, Edinburgh to succeed Gordon Powell – thence on to journey's end at Tullimarine Airport, Melbourne, to a large welcoming party, including the Powells, and the new Chairman of the Turnbull Trustees, Werner Brodbeck, a very skilful Swiss business man; along with his delightful wife, Priska, we became great friends. Next day we went to see Scots Church, a fine building, seating 900. It was built over a hundred years ago; the winning tender was for £19,999 19s 6d, and was carried out by a Scot, Willie Mitchell, who lived in a house called Coldstream. He had a daughter called Nellie, who sang in Scots' Choir, and when she developed a professional career she called herself Nellie Melba, from Melbourne, to the lasting regret of millions of peaches. Mitchell was a bit ordinary for anyone making for fame.

After a few days in the Windsor Hotel, solidly old-fashioned, we settled into the headmaster's house at Haileybury Junior School, Brighton. He and his wife were over in Scotland for the wedding of their daughter. We were very comfortable and well looked after, with logs from the School, a kindly home help, and the oversight of the bursar. It was ten miles from the centre, so I was given the use of a rented car, an Escort: the first car caused no end of trouble, and had to be changed for a new one, which was a hideous tomato ketchup colour. We were usually driven to Church on Sundays and Wednesdays by a kindly couple, Es and Jessie Hines. The Services, both Morning and Evening were well-filled, though nothing like Sydney. The Morning was recorded in full and broadcast later. The Choir always sang two anthems, which made the Service long and overloaded – at a later date I got on to preach at 7.50, the Service having started at 7.00! I met, and long enjoyed, the friendship of the Associate, Ray Russell, known affectionately as 'Bish'! He had been a Principal Chaplain in the RAAF; he did most of the pastoral work, preparing of First Communicants, etc.

He was a great character and a wonderful friend. He had a wonderful story about crossing from New York on the *Queen Mary* with 12,000 Aussie and American service-men. They had no convoy, and relied on her speed alone, constantly zig-zagging. Now they were in the sheltered waters of the Clyde, and Bish found himself beside an American major, looking out on the lush pastures of Ayrshire. Reflectively the major remarked: 'I wonder when the British will get down to building a ship like this?' More in sorrow than in anger Bish took him by the arm, and led him to the landing of the 1st Class dining saloon, where hung a life-size portrait of HM Queen Mary with a brass plaque, which he asked the American to read: 'This ship was launched on the Clyde by Her Majesty Queen Mary on . . .' – still mystified the major asked: 'So, where is this Clyde they're talking about?'

Quite early on we had a TV Service, in which I spoke to the children about a tea towel depicting both Forth Bridges; then the children went out, processing up the centre aisle, straight into camera. One family, father, mother and four children, walked towards me smiling broadly and looking familiar. I had confirmed and married the parents, and christened all four children in St. Cuthbert's . . . this kind of thing happened constantly. After three weeks I got a phone call from the Matron of the Jessie Macpherson Memorial Hospital:

'Dr Small, I have a patient here who claims to be a member of your Church.'

'You mean Scots Kirk?'

'No, no, St. Cuthbert's.'

In I went – here's this buxom Scots body sitting up in bed, and delighted to see me.

'Mrs Myles, I thought you lived just off Leith Walk.'

'Aye, so we did: we came out here eighteen months ago, just forgot to tell ye.'

'Well, I've gone a long way to visit my members in hospital, 10,000 miles beats a'.'

In addition to meeting old friends like this we made many new ones. One family in particular became close friends, and we went with them. John Colvin was a skilled eye surgeon, originally from Tasmania, who trained in Edinburgh in the Eye Pavilion, then went on to Leeds Infirmary where he met and married Sylvia, who was nursing. He was also a pilot in the RAAF, and had been closely associated with NASA in preparation for the space flights; he had been instrumental in perfecting the special material used in the 'windows' of the space suits: unbreakable, unscratchable, does not mist up. He gave me some marvellous photographs from outer space, even taken on the moon. He and Sylvia had three children, David, Alan, and Andrea, a tot of just four.

They were all daft about Australian Rules Football. It is an extraordinary game, the most popular spectator sport in Australia, so I must attempt to describe it. It is played with eighteen players a side, on a circular pitch as large as Melbourne Cricket Ground. At each end are two sets of goalposts, the inner ones as tall as rugby posts, the outer much shorter; a ball kicked between the outer posts is a 'behind' and scores 1, between the centre posts is a goal and counts 6.

The game starts with the umpire bouncing the ball on the centre spot; players then jump for it like basketball; you can kick it, pass, punch it, knock it on any way; a clean catch overhead is like a 'mark', and you get a free kick at the ball; the idea is to get a mark near enough to the opponents' goal to get a clear kick and score. You can tackle any way except barging and pushing, and there are no scrums. If the ball goes out of play the touch judge throws it in, turning his back to the play and throwing it high and backwards over his head. There are now two field umpires, two touch judges, and two goal umpires, who signal with flags when a goal or a behind is scored. It is a very fast game; there are four quarters of twenty-five minutes; five minutes interval between each quarter, and fifteen minutes half-time. It is hugely popular – 120,000 at the Grand Final is normal. The youngsters take it very seriously; during the week they will make a huge plastic banner: HAWKS FOR THE CUP. The team runs through this. There is fierce local loyalty, each suburb having its team.

The Colvins' team was Hawthorn, known as The Hawks, and it became ours. By the time we had got really keen I preached a children's sermon on 'Support the team, and wear the colours', asking why they should make such a fuss about a football team, but not be proud of belonging to the team of Jesus. I then said: 'I'm going to show you I'm not ashamed of the team I barrack for', took up a big orange and gold Hawthorn scarf and wound it twice round my neck – laughter, cheers and boos from the congregation! A journalist who happened to be in Church wrote an article for the evening paper about the Minister who got booed in Church! The Hawthorn directors took it up, invited me to lunch before one of their big games, and made me an Honorary Life Member.

Having declared and explained this special connection with Australian Rules Football, it dawns on me that I am in a peculiar position to compare and comment on the various forms of the game which goes by the generic name of 'football'. Only one is played with a ball that is shaped like one,

Honorary member of 'The Hawks': Australian Rules Football Club 'Hawthorn'. With Sylvia Colvin. Rug made for RLS by old supporter

Association or soccer. That form I have played at various levels, and watched often, both live and on TV. Rugby League I have also seen, both live in Sydney, where it is the main spectator sport, and on Grandstand on TV. Rugby Union has gradually become my main interest through my boys going to Watson's, from the time in 1951 when Ronald first played for the School. This interest went on to the next generation, when I had seven grandsons playing on a Saturday morning. The next stage came when Niall, Ronald's eldest, played in the Schools International against France and Wales, and for Watsonians and Edinburgh under-21. At a later stage there was a period when Ronald was chairman of the team selection committee, Colin was (and still is) the club doctor, Catriona was handling catering in the Pavilion after the matches, and her husband, Graham, held the joint record for games played with the Club. In addition, I have been for twenty-five years chaplain to the Co-optomist Rugby Club. As a 'heretic' I have retained my critical faculties, so let's begin with Rugby Union.

The first time I saw a rugby match I was bewildered by sixteen men pushing against each other, like a couple of crabs with extra legs fighting a mating duel: I am still bewildered and concerned. I pay £18 for a stand ticket at Murrayfield to see eighty minutes of play, and, according to a recent estimate, I get about twenty minutes of the ball actually in play. I am very concerned about the sheer waste of time spent getting the scrum straight, getting it up when it has collapsed, getting it back to 'the mark'. I am much more concerned about the skullduggery that goes on in and around the scrum; the heavy packs that charge into their opponents, and shove before the ball is ready to be put in; between that and pulling down, I am amazed that there are not more serious injuries. But that is nothing to what goes on in the scrum. It is significant that David Sole should appear to play in a certain International with no sleeves on his jersey! If I may be personal, when my eldest grandson, Niall, was playing hooker for Watsonians, aged nineteen, against another Edinburgh team, he came off halfway through the second half to have his cheek stitched, for the opposing prop had bitten a piece out of it! Now, it is flattering to know that the genes have produced in another generation such succulent and desirable flesh, but this is a bit much (no pun intended). When the Watsonian committee protested, it was brushed aside: 'There was a lot of biting going on in the front row.' Still on the pack, I find it increasingly bad for the game that emphasis is being laid, more and more, on huge forwards, with height, weight, and 'upper body strength', and the tendency that goes with it to 'play the game tight'. That, of course, goes with the motivation to win at all costs.

I have long advocated some form of differential penalty. Far too many games are won on penalty kicks, often for minor or technical offences, or infringements it is almost impossible to avoid. If you are tackled and the ball goes to ground, you are supposed to roll clear and make the ball available, but how on earth can you do that, with at least three opponents already on top of you? I find it all wrong that the same penalty should be imposed for an offence of that kind, as for raking a player with your boot, stamping, or punching. For a blatant foul of the latter nature I would follow Soccer, and have a penalty in front of the posts, no matter where the offence occurs. I get hot under the collar over the 'off the ball' ugly fouls, and welcome the intervention of touch judges at top level. I feel the same about the uneven standards of discipline and punishment operated by different countries. I cannot understand how some countries go on picking a player who can do that kind of thing, after a ridiculously brief suspension. I am also against the many forms of gamesmanship, like the dummy pass from the scrum, in which the former English scrum half, Richard Hill, specialises. I am glad to see the International Board have heard my cry, and stopped some of the abuses of the game which spoil it as a spectacle.

Concerning Rugby League I cannot say nearly as much. It is an increasingly popular sport, but I know it only as a casual, and usually TV, spectator. It seems to me to be like the little girl who had a curl that grew in the middle of her forehead – when it is good, it is very, very good, but when it is bad, it is horrid. The close tackling, the heeling back, can lead to constant, annoying stoppages, leaving little room for open back play, which can be so thrilling. The scrums are weird and wonderful; the scrum half throws the ball in like a guided missile. The standards of skill, passing, fielding, kicking, seem to me to be on the whole better than in Union. The strictness of the refereeing cuts down the kind of offences I have been complaining about. This, by the way, is to me one of the main defects of Australian Rules. It is a contact sport, and rammies, punch-ups, etc., are frequent. When that happens, all thirty-six players join in, along with the six umpires, and even the mounted police who ride the range! Then when the huddle is all sorted out the umpire bounces the ball and we start again. He has no power to send anyone off; he can put a player 'on report', his case will be tried by a tribunal, and he may be suspended. One of the first games I saw was kind of 'towsy', and I said to John Colvin: 'I would have sent off about four players on each side; then we could have got on with the game!'

That leaves my beloved and much lamented soccer. The first senior game I ever saw as a schoolboy was at Tynecastle; the Scottish League v the Irish

League. The Scottish left wing consisted of Patsy Gallacher of Celtic and Alan Morton of Rangers. Wee Patsy, a typical product of industrial Glasgow, trained with a tanner ba' on the back greens of the tenements, could make the ball talk, he dribbled as if it were tied to his shoelaces; Alan could swing over one of those hanging crosses that curled beyond the defence and landed in the far end of the six-yard box, true to an inch to the incoming forward's head. I thought it was fascinating, and I sigh for it still. I am left bewildered and exasperated by the modern game, passing across, passing back, often from ridiculous distances; thank goodness, no one ever passed back to me from near the centre spot! This slow build-up, as if you were playing a game of chess, seems to me to be spoiling the game as a spectacle. But most alarming of all is the hideous over-commercialisation of the game. I cannot believe that any player is worth a million pounds or more. Players get delusions of grandeur about their importance in the scheme of things. The fact that I am a Hearts supporter has no connection with my inability to rejoice in Rangers' continued success, for the simple reason that it boosts the idea which is the curse of our materialistic society, namely that money will buy anything. A propos of Leeds United winning the English League, I got out the old photo of the game in which I played at Elland Road, and the obvious feature was that almost every man was wearing a cloth cap. The way the game is going it is pricing out his equivalent, and that I bitterly regret.

It is time to go back on to Church Services. Attendances continued to grow till they had to bring in extra chairs, and still have people standing, and this just went on. On one occasion we had an official visit by the Governor of Victoria, Sir Rohan Delacombe. When I went to meet him at the door, he said: 'My son is an officer in the Royal Scots – he's just been posted to Edinburgh Castle, and he looks down on your Church every day when he goes to his office.' In between Services we managed several trips, near or far. Although it was mid-winter kind friends organised many delightful picnics. On 21 June we had a great picnic, sitting in the open, near Eildon Dam, which Ray Mason, one of our company of friends had a big hand in building. It is 260' high, 3,225' long, and contains seventeen million tons of earth and rock. It has a shore-line of three hundred miles!

With the Colvin family we took one of our many short term excursions, first out to Mt. Dandenong to visit the William Ricketts Sanctuary: he is a man who lived among the aborigines, and adopted their belief that all life is spirit, and their reverence for life. He has produced most astonishing sculptures in clay, figures of human beings, birds, animals, set out in an area of woodland. From there to Sir Colin Mackenzie Sanctuary. He was a famous naturalist who left this great area, where people could see, as we did, the animals in natural conditions, kangaroos, wombats, emus, and the highlight of it all, the lyre-bird doing its courting display, with that marvellous tail. We also saw that strangest member of the animal race, the platypus, and were astonished it was so small.

For a longer trip Bish and Eileen Russell took us to their country cottage on Phillip Island far south, on a hill called Wimbledon Estate, with every road named from a famous Wimbledon player, e.g. Hoad Road and Rosewall Crescent. There they left us to drive down that evening and again next morning to see the fairy penguins, coming home from the fishing and setting out again. These quaint little creatures come out of the surf, wait till they have a sort of quorum, then come chattering up the beach, laden with their haul of pre-digested fish. On the way home I had an unhappy new experience – a passing truck kicked up a stone which shattered my windscreen, leaving me with about two square inches to peer through. Under these conditions I crawled some twenty-five miles, till I found a garage that could replace the screen. The young chap who did it told me his mother came from Hawick, his father from Cowdenbeath. Apparently this shattered screen is a common occurrence – indeed there is a road in Queensland called The Crystal Highway because of the piles of glass, where drivers have done the right thing and smashed out the broken screen.

Another trip, on a cold day, took us to Ballarat, where first we visited the site of Eureka Fort, the scene of the only battle on Australian soil. Back in 1851 the miners revolted against the injustices of the government and lack of representation and barricaded themselves in a very primitive stockade on the top of a small hill. The troops were called in and there was a massacre, but public opinion was shocked and the miners gained their point. We then went to visit the old mine workings, now being restored. It all began with a gold strike in a little creek, now running through the heart of the city, and then gold was found in the quartz on the hill. They have restored the old pit-gear, many of the shops, the bank, a Chinese joss-house and restaurant and small mines. There were two horses working, one at a grinding mill, and the other operating a hoist. You can still 'pan' for gold but you won't get very rich. Ballarat is also famous for a gorgeous begonia show, which we saw on a later visit.

During our three months in Melbourne we were allowed the inside of two weeks for longer absences. We paid a visit to Adelaide, staying with Ian Tanner and his family, and taking a special Service in St. Andrew's Church. While we were there he got word that he had been chosen as the next Moderator of the Presbyterian Church of South Australia, and we were, of course, full of congratulations. 'Look,' he said, 'Don't take it too seriously; it's only thirty-four congregations. In Scotland it wouldn't be even a sizeable Presbytery!' We sometimes forget the vast differences, and the status of being the National Church. We found Adelaide a beautiful city, imaginatively laid out, and not yet too large.

Beyond doubt the most memorable 'outside' visit was the one we paid to Broken Hill, that strange mining town, totally ruled by the unions. We went there because the local minister was Campbell Egan, who had been my Assistant in 1966, and whose daughter Catriona I had christened. His uncle was the Royal Flying Doctor based on Broken Hill, and he had arranged for me to go out on patrol. This was a great thrill. We flew in a Beagle aircraft with twin RR engines, and room for the pilot, duty doctor, nurse, patient, on a stretcher if need be, and a companion. The first station at which we landed had gathered fifteen patients, from a baby getting an inoculation to an old man having an injection for a heart condition. It had a generator, so enjoyed all mod cons. The son of the owner was there with his attractive, mini-skirted wife. I said to him:

'As a matter of interest, what do you do here for girl friends?'

'Oh,' he replied, 'There wasn't much competition. She was our next-door neighbour.'

'What does that mean?'

'She was only fifty miles away!'

I was asked to go in and visit the old granny. Here she was, sitting up in bed with a helio hairwash for the occasion, with the famous devotional book *Daily Light* at her bedside, and listening in to Dr Finlay's Casebook on the radio – Mrs Foggo from Braemar aged ninety-one.

At 5.00 p.m., we sat in the base hospital and listened in to the Clinic of the Air, when the people of the Outback, using their transceiver sets, reported on patients and their symptoms. One in particular did my heart good. Voice over the ether:

'Eh! doctor, I'm awfu' worried aboot my laddie. He's got horrid sores a' aboot his mooth, they're right nasty.'

Doctor: 'Are they wet sores or dry sores?'

'Haud on a meenit and I'll look; he's running aboot in the yard.'

Slight pause while, three hundred miles away she takes a look, then comes back:

'They're wet sores . . . right nasty.'

'Right' says the doctor, 'he's got impetigo; you'll touch them with lotion 89, and give him two pills a day of bottle 31 in your medicine chest.'

It's a wonderful system; it does away with children suffering, even dying, because no one knew what to do. In an emergency the out-station puts on its distinctive call sign; that activates the pilot, duty doctor and nurse. If you can guarantee a strip 100 yards x 30 yards, over which you can drive an ordinary car at 30 m.p.h. without discomfort, and no stray stock, they will land any time day or night, and get a patient into hospital quicker than from the outskirts of Melbourne. After the clinic, they read the telegrams, so everyone knows what is happening to everyone else. It has certainly banished solitariness; they call it the 'galah session' a galah being a very chattersome Australian parrot!

I met there a very wonderful young woman; a keen sportswoman, at eighteen she was flung from her horse, and became a paraplegic. Using the School of the Air network, she runs a Sunday School of the Air. I recorded for her two programmes about the carving of 'The Last Supper' and 'The Relics of St. Cuthbert'. Another interesting feature of the Broken Hill week was a visit we paid to a special small community at Menindee Dam, with waterworks and about eighty people. There were three Methodist deaconesses; one taught school and took Services while the other two were nurses and ran the little hospital. When we were leaving I said to the senior Sister how much I admired this unusual work they were doing.

'You ought to,' she replied, 'for you sent me here.'

'What on earth do you mean?'

'Well, back in 1962 I had finished my training, and had no idea how to use it. I went to an Evening Service in St. Stephen's, Sydney, and you preached a sermon that sent me here.'

That brings me back to the Church Services, which all this time just kept on growing. The climax came at the early August Communion, near the end of the Turnbull Trust Ministry. They knew they were going to have problems with numbers, so they borrowed trays and glasses from neighbouring Churches. Even at that they were so nearly 'out' that there were no glasses for the duty elders sitting round behind the Table. With carefully suppressed glee I served them with the two big common cups on the Table 'for decoration', and they had to take them! We were at the Manse for lunch, and Gordon was in a state of great excitement: 'If only two hundred turn up tonight, it's a record.' In fact five hundred turned up, and Gordon claimed it was an all-time record for any Church in Australia, which would be difficult to prove or disprove, if you think of several RC masses. Anyway I asked him for the actual numbers.

'1746.'

'Great,' I said, 'Very easy to remember. That's the date of the Battle of Culloden!'

Interior of Scots Church, Melbourne, Communion Sunday. Here record attendance of 1746 at Communion, August 1971

Apart from all these special occasions there were all sorts of less spectacular activities – radio and TV interviews and programmes, talks to groups of ministers or church folk. Very specially an address to Scotch College, founded by the Presbyterian Church; the first five principals from Scotland, the first two from Aberdeen . . . a truly great School, with high standards and widespread prestige. On a very personal note – on 22 June we celebrated our Ruby Wedding, and received this cable from our iniquitous family: 'HAPPY RUBY WEDDING FROM YOUR 45 YEAR OLD FAMILY'.

It will be gathered from the above record that Jean enjoyed comparatively good health, and was able to move about with surprising freedom. She was very well looked after by a senior neurologist, Dr Graham Robertson, to whom her own Professor, John Gillingham, had recommended her. He took great trouble with her case, being most particular about her drugs and the exact dosage. He was an expert on the ornamental iron-work with which so many of the older houses were decorated. Unhappily he died of cancer at Christmas 1975, just before our next visit, to which, as will shortly emerge, his knowledge and skill would have made a blessed difference.

When it came to leaving we took an unusual route home. We flew to Perth, and had a brief stop-over with the parents of Joan Macfarlane, wife of my Associate, Alwyn. We then flew South African Airways to Johannesburg, stopping to refuel at Mauritius. At Jo'burg we found to our pleased surprise that SAS regarded us as passengers in transit, and paid for a taxi to the hotel (which we had already booked), all hotel expenses, and a taxi back to the airport next morning – we were most impressed. In Cape Town we stayed out at Sea Point, in a comfortable hotel whose manageress came from Edinburgh; we managed in a couple of days to see most of the sights and, in spite of my fear of heights, went to the top of Table Mountain. There were several little indications of apartheid – separate windows for buying stamps in the GPO, buses upstairs black, downstairs white; even separate toilets on top of Table Mountain!

On 15 September we boarded the Union Castle liner SS *Vaal* – she was quite a ship, 30,212 tons, 760′ long, 90′ in the beam. She can carry 725 passengers, but was by no means full. We had a comfortable cabin and a comfortable voyage, just lying in the sun, reading and relaxing after a pretty hectic three months. The highlight was, of course, Crossing the Line, which we had done three times before. There was no lack of gaiety about King Neptune and his court. He had a wonderful wife, Aphrodite, with balloons as bosom. They put the children through first, very kindly. There were then five 'victims', including three girls. They were each dealt with by the 'surgeon' and his team; anaesthetised with two whacks on the table with a mallet, operated on with a large saw and a bloody knife. Various 'organs' were removed, sausages and sundry gory items. One man had a string of light bulbs removed, and from one of the girls a bra and a pair of panties. Very funny was a chap in oilskins, sea-boots and souwester who kept marching down into the pool with a tiny plastic pail and going emptying it over the side. After a brief call at Las Palmas we landed at Southampton, caught the boat train, the shuttle, and so Hume sweet Hume!

By 1976 I had retired, and my time was my own, so when I was invited to be Turnbull Trust Preacher for the second time, we planned to do a leisurely round-the-world trip, going out by South Africa, and home by Canada. A lot had changed at both ends, even in five years. Jean's disability had considerably increased – she was in process of being stabilised on a new drug, Sinemet, which was a great improvement on the original rather crude L dopa; you could get the same results with one-fifth the amount. The Presbyterian Church in Australia had gone through the trauma of the badly bungled Union with the Methodist and Congregational Churches. There had been much bitterness, and the usual lawsuits about property, the

Presbyterian Church, typically, having so many of the best schools and
hospitals. St. Stephen's, Sydney, on the first vote, chose to stay Presbyterian; on the second, held a year later, it changed its mind and went into
the Uniting Church. Scots Melbourne remained staunchly Presbyterian.
Gordon Powell had been determined on Union; he went so far as to issue an
ultimatum just before they voted: 'Either you vote for Union, or I will leave
you.' They 'called his bluff', and he duly left, going to a fabulously wealthy
Church in the USA: 'Christ's Church on Quaker Hill'. Scots were therefore
in the throes of an awkward vacancy, wondering if they should give up
trying to get a minister from Scotland, and look instead, say, to
Canada.

We left home on 22 January by train, spent a night in London with Ben
and Ismay Davies, whom I had married in Cramond, and got the boat train
to Southampton, where we boarded again the *Vaal*. We had the company at
table, irregularly, of Gordon Stone, one of my old Cramond Scouts, now a
big business man – he did not often appear at breakfast! We had a kind and
helpful waitress, Anita, who cut up Jean's food for her. It was an uneventful
voyage, and let us do our acclimatisation gradually. One thing we noticed –
everything was a little sub-standard since 1971, food and service, not quite
so good; they were even economising on oil fuel, so the ship's run instead of
550 miles a day was about 485. When we got to Cape Town we were met by
Anne Grieve, daughter of Lord Grieve, one of my elders. I had married her
to a South African just weeks before. She saw us on to the plane to
Johannesburg, where we were met by Mannie van Heerden, who was to be
our host for the next week. He and his wife had worshipped at St.
Cuthbert's during the Festival, and insisted that we had a week's stop-over
with them. He ran a shirt-selling business, and had a beautiful home, in one
and a half acres of ground, with tennis court and swimming pool. We met
his wife, Elveleen, two boys, Karl, twelve, Alfred, ten, and a little girl of
three and a half, who knew nothing but Afrikaans, and screamed and threw
a strum, because she could not communicate! After our evening meal we
had family worship, still sitting round the table. Mannie read a passage
from Acts in Afrikaans, I said a prayer in English, they sang a hymn in
Afrikaans – a typical devout Dutch Reformed family, combining this
sincere worship with the OT idea that God has appointed some people to be
hewers of wood and drawers of water. Next morning an official from the
Ministry of the Interior showed me over the township of Soweto, Mannie
having been hurt by a BBC2 programme which he said was unfair to what
they do for the blacks. I was not impressed by what they do in segregating
600,000 (more likely a million) in terms of colour. There was a wonderful

Baragwanath Hospital, so named for the Cornish farmer who had owned the site, which they claim is the largest hospital in the southern hemisphere. It certainly does splendid work, largely among mothers and babies. When in hospital they teach the patients to eat fish, and to accept brown bread, which the African thinks must be inferior because it isn't white!

On the Sunday I preached in the morning in St. Columba's Presbyterian Church, which admits no colour bar – a strong congregation, with 1,600 members, and 400 in the Sunday School. It was very interesting because when we had been three years in Bathgate, I was asked to go to that Church, but declined because Jean read of a thunderstorm with hailstones as big as pigeons' eggs. Just to prove her wisdom we had two thunder storms, the worst I have ever known. Next week we drove 250 miles to the Kruger Game Park, where we were to spend two nights. We saw all sorts of animals, totally tame, because all protected, but no lions or elephants. The following day we had a very long drive because of flooding and bridges down, in terrific heat. Jean went down with heatstroke which, combined with her main illness, made her very ill, and there was no doctor for miles. Fortunately Elveleen had done some special training in First Aid, and with ice packs and cold washes got her temperature down, but it was very unfortunate.

On the flight to Melbourne next day she went to the other extreme, sleeping under the air vent. We had arranged to exchange houses with Bill and Libba Brown in 43 Power Street, and for the next few days till they left Mrs Marjory McKay, widow of Cecil McKay of Sunshine Harvester fame, had kindly asked us to stay in the self-contained flat of her house in Toorak. Jean was clearly very ill, and we called in Dr Diggle, whose father had been a great friend of Prof. J.S. Stewart. It turned out that, on top of everything else, she now had pneumonia. Once she got over that she was still not right, vomiting because of the drugs, and frequently falling. She was put in the charge of the neurologist who had taken over Dr Robertson's cases, and had her notes from 1971. He put her back on the crude L dopa, and a larger dose, so she just could not sleep, in spite of the several sleeping pills he prescribed. The meticulous diary I was keeping every morning starts: 'Did not sleep at all; up several times to toilet or being sick; shook all night'. It really was a very trying situation for her, and for me, because the Church attendances were as before, and very demanding. Friends were very kind, coming in to 'granny-sit' or taking her to their home, as the Colvins did in particular, thus letting me get to Church or to some necessary outside engagement.

She was taken into a private hospital, run by the Tramway Department, very expensive, and not very efficient. The first morning I went in just in time to stop a Burmese nursing sister giving her an increased dose of her drug, instead of reducing it, which was the object of the exercise. Plans were set on foot to get her moved to St. Andrew's Presbyterian Hospital. On Wednesday, just before I went into the Service, I got a message that straight after I was go to and move her. I took the Service under some understandable stress; we ended by singing 'O love that wilt not let me go', No. 424 in the Revised Church Hymnary. I went out and picked her up from the tramway hospital and took her to St. Andrew's, where she was received by the Assistant Matron, wheeled upstairs, and into a four-bed ward – the number on the door: 424! I took it as a symbol of hope. She made steady progress, not least in her general vitality and spirit. Very kindly the directors refused to make any charge for her time in hospital 'in view of all that I had done for the Church'. Although she was considerably better, she was still vulnerable. One afternoon I went out, leaving the key for my old Assistant, John Cleghorn, to get in. When he arrived he found her sitting on a chair in the hall, with the grandfather clock on top of her. She had got up to go to the toilet, fallen and landed on the chair, knocking into the clock in the process. It was lying at an angle, the top dug into the plaster, and the glass almost touching her face! In spite of the degree of improvement it was quite clear that our round trip plans had to be cancelled. This proved very difficult. I was told by Cooks that the refund for our cancelled tickets could only be paid in sterling after we got home, and I had to pay 1,234 dollars that week. I was shattered – that on top of everything else. Fortunately Werner Brodbeck heard of my plight, and hastened to assure me the Trustees still had to pay me $2,000 – they had increased the allowance without telling me. As the end of our time in Melbourne drew near the Trustees gave a lovely dinner, for the two of us, all the Trustees, and friends like John and Sylvia Colvin who had been so understanding and helpful.

We had a moving farewell as we flew to Sydney, where we stayed with Jean and Albert Himmelhoch. He had obtained a supply of Sinemet, gave her a mild dose, and minimal sleeping pills, and she slept very well. We saw the neurologist, Dr George Selby, who had looked after her in 1971. He heard the whole story, examined her carefully, and concluded that the whole traumatic experience was due to the overdose of L dopa, which her body refused to tolerate. I left her in charge of Jean and Albert and flew first to Wellington, where I stayed with my brother Colin, his wife, Wenda, and their two delightful youngsters, Helen and Keith. We also drove 100 kms. to Lake Alice Hospital to visit my older sister, Winifred, a retired doctor, now a permanent resident there. She was in surprisingly good form, asking about all the family, mentally clear as a bell. For the weekend I flew to Christchurch, staying with cousin Burness Niven; then travelled down to Dunedin, where I preached in Knox Church after a gap of twenty-six years. After the Morning Service we had a delightful reunion with twenty-one of Jean's relations – it was such a pity she could not be there. Then it was back to Sydney, final packing, then off for home. Qantas were very helpful, giving us the front two seats in economy, with access to the 1st class toilet, and permission to use it, which was a great help. At Heathrow they laid on not only a chair, but an estate car to transfer us to the shuttle for Edinburgh. How either of us survived that experience, looking back now, I can never understand. It made for a somewhat unhappy final visit.

That, in the event, it turned out not to be. Just before Christmas 1978, I had a phone call from Melbourne, asking if I could go out, even for a shorter period, as a last-minute replacement for John R. Gray. I at once replied: 'No way – my wife's at the wheel-chair stage!'

'Well, don't refuse us now. Think about it and we'll phone you again tomorrow . . . we would do anything to make it possible.'

I took Jean to her day hospital as usual, saying nothing to her. I got hold of Professor Williamson, her chief, and told him.

'Frankly, at the stage she is at now, physically it will make little difference; the mental tonic would be good, depending on how she takes it.'

I collected Catriona for support, picked Jean up and, rather tentatively, broke the news.

'What a grand idea,' she replied, 'When do we leave?'

In a few weeks we were off, by 24 February. We went first to Oxford and stayed with Robert and Alison Duthie. She was the daughter of the Headmaster of Cargilfield, and theirs was the last wedding I had in Cramond. Robert is now the Professor of Orthopaedic Surgery in the Nuffield Unit at Oxford. Next day Alison drove us to Heathrow, just an hour away, so that we started fresh.

Qantas gave us the same facilities as before. We got off and walked at Bahrein and Singapore, and arrived not too tired, having had room to lie down and sleep. Jean was put straight into St. Andrew's Hospital to recuperate, which she did very successfully. She got a chit: 'To cost of laundry during the period of your confinement'! I was put up for the few days in the Victoria Hotel, where I spent most of the time in the refuge of my room, as the hotel was infested by white-clad women bowlers from all over! After about a week we moved into Broadmead, a residential home for the elderly, run by the Methodist Church, where Jean had gone for therapy in 1976. We had two rooms, comfortably furnished, with mod. cons., and bathroom only yards away. All meals were served in the dining room, and we were given a thermos of Milo for late evening. I could go out to an evening engagement and know that the night sister would have Jean duly bathed, in bed and probably asleep. It worked very well; we still had our bad nights – twice she fell out of bed – but she was better able to get about during the day. She managed the Morning Service most Sundays, sitting in the front pew with June Martin and Sylvia Colvin on either side, like heraldic 'supporters'; she managed to get to Test matches and the first Military Tattoo, to several barbecues and dinner parties, to a trip to the safari park at Mt. Macedon.

Scots was going through a difficult time with another vacancy. Max Putmam, whom they had called from Canada on the strength of exchanged tapes, had not proved a success, and after two years had just up-tailed and gone home. I sat in early on at a meeting of their Vacancy Committee of fifteen. I spoke for over thirty minutes on the need to face their situation, with all the problems of a centre city congregation of a minority Church, and tried to get them to accept Norman Pritchard, who had been three years Assistant in St. George's West and shown great promise. When the Interim Moderator asked for questions or comments I couldn't believe my ears. One man said he was too young, he wouldn't be able to preach till he was fifty! A woman, studying Norman's curriculum vitae, picked out a plum: 'Oh! we can't have him. He trained under Willie Barclay – he's contaminated!'!! They got themselves into an unholy mess, with the extreme right wingers protesting to the Presbytery about the procedure; the net result was that a Congregational Meeting was called to come to a decision. It was moved that they invite Norman to come out 'on appro'. Someone else got up and said: 'Leonard Small knows us better than anyone else – he knows this young man well; if he thinks this is the right man for us, I move we call him with no more fuss.' This was carried by a huge majority, and Norman and Joan duly came out, and he has done an outstanding job.

In spite of all this argumentation and stress the attendances at all Services remained encouragingly good with much fine singing by the congregation; at the Lunch Hour Service the men's Choir were still leading nobly. There were a variety of 'outside jobs'. I went to Geelong for a special Service – a city of 120,000 inhabitants, with a famous School where Prince Charles was a pupil. I spoke on Good Friday to the pupils of Carey Grammar School about the meaning of the Cross. After having attended a performance of the first ever Melbourne Military Tattoo, I went back and did the Epilogue at the end of the closing performance, coming on after the massed bands played and 27,000 people sang Amazing Grace – quite an experience. I attended a Reception, given jointly by the Uniting and Presbyterian Churches, for the Moderator of the Presbyterian Church of the New Hebrides, the Principal of a High School, a woman representative of their PWMU, and an organiser of rural pastorates. It was marvellous to hear them talking about their work, and to remember their grandparents were cannibals! I was also interested to learn that they used tapes of my Sydney sermons on the small islands where they cannot get a preacher.

Most outstanding of all was our visit to Wagga Wagga, where Campbell Egan had moved from Artarmon in Sydney. In geography at school I used to imagine that Wagga Wagga must be the original 'hick town'. It is actually a beautiful city, laid out round a lagoon and ornamental parks. Campbell had laid on a Service for Churches of all sorts for fifty miles around, and involved the Mayor and Council. There was a huge turn out, and we were led in by two buxom women pipers! We travelled very comfortably by train, seeing some fine pastoral country. I also regularly took the Wednesday morning Service in Broadmead – incidentally our table companions were a retired Methodist minister and his wife, 91 and 90 respectively; he was deaf and she was blind, but he said that between his eyes and her ears they managed fine! This very extra special visit drew to a moving close with a wonderful Service on Good Friday, and a first class TV Service on Easter Day. So, having arrived on 26 February we left for Sydney on 17 April.

We went and stayed at Killara, as usual, finding the Himmelhoch family all, of course, three years older, and at various stages in their studies. We had deliberately arranged not to stay more than two or three weeks, so I took nothing more than symbolic services in St. Stephen's. There was a particularly happy occasion when I christened a baby called Neil Fraser. I had married his parents Robin and Margaret (Margaret had been Colin's theatre sister in the Simpson). I married them in St. Cuthbert's on 8 August one year, and on the same date the following year met them in St. Stephen's. They brought their daughter, Julie, home to be christened, but Neil was done in 'foreign parts'. When the few days of renewing contact with old friends were ended, we made for home, because Jean, by this time, was getting weary. We had a good trip home, Qantas again providing all possible help, and arrived home after a wonderful and encouraging experience – all the more encouraging because it had seemed so unlikely. It gave to Jean and myself and all our close friends in Australia an extra wealth of happy memories. If you can have an Indian summer in Australia then we had it. Looking ahead, when Jean died in October of that same year both St. Stephen's and Scots Church put identical In Memoriam notices in their principal newspapers: 'In loving and grateful memory of Jean, wife of the Very Rev. Dr. L. Small – a very gallant Lady.'

Chapter 13

Moderator

Functioning for a year as Moderator of the General Assembly is a thrilling and unforgettable experience. Just after the end of my year a godly lady said to me, with very sincere sympathy: 'It must have been a dreadful strain; I don't know how you could stand it.' I replied, a little unappreciatively: 'On the contrary, I enjoyed every minute of it!' Just accepting the tremendous privilege and responsibility, taking one's place in the long line of tradition back to giants like Andrew Melville and John Knox (yet again), so wonderfully belonging in a challenging heritage – who would not be humbled yet thrilled? As I took the chair, and accepted the ring, which is passed on as a kind of badge of office, I had a 'flashback' to my father being shouted down in that same building, and wondered if, from among the Communion of Saints, 'he saw of the travail of his soul and was satisfied.' Chairing the Assembly itself was challenging, keeping the business going without being 'bossy', looking out for the character who came forward saying: 'Moderator, I had no intention of speaking,' and then produced typewritten notes; or the other who got up to ask a question, and then made a speech.

It was a special responsibility to handle worthily the special occasions, like thanking Professor J.S. Stewart on his retirement (he got a standing ovation). It was not necessary in his case, but in others it was worthwhile doing one's homework, so as to make the tribute personal and adequate. In those days the Assembly lasted for ten days. Near the end of the first week Lord Strachan, our senior Elder, and former Procurator, said to me: 'I must admire the way you are handling the business; you let people have their say without going on too long; you seem to sense when the Assembly is ready to come to a decision, so we get through without either dragging or rushing.' I replied, wickedly, 'Lord Strachan, I've had ten years' experience as Moderator of the Kirk Session of St. Cuthbert's.'

In the visitation of Presbyteries, under the ten-year rota, I did Melrose, Dumfries, Haddington and Dunbar, Moray, Glasgow and Cupar. They were all different, and have left their differing abiding impressions. In the country, talking to the farmers in the auction mart was testing, in Elgin it was hilarious. They had forgotten we were coming; the auctioneer simply

Moderator, in the chair of the Assembly

banged on his desk and shouted; 'Moderator of the General Assembly wants to speak to you chaps,' whereupon they opened a hurdle and ushered into the ring in front of me three black stirks, mooing and bawling . . . the most unresponsive congregation I ever had! I was able to break down the apathy of the faces around me by saying: 'I must be the only Moderator who has been dipped in sheep dip,' and went on to describe how, working as a Scout on a farm at Castle Douglas we had been dipping sheep. I was given the job of pushing their heads under with a forked stick. I was getting tired and losing my concentration, so I missed and fell in beside a big old ewe. As my rude family say: 'And as usual, Dad, your mouth would be open.' I can taste it yet! I also told them of the Minister in the country, all of whose congregation were working on the land. They came in from the open air and the atmosphere of the kirk was soporific, so they just went to sleep on him. He decided to put a stop to this, so he worked out a scheme whereby, every three minutes during his sermon, he banged the pulpit and exclaimed: 'God grant,' and at the word 'grant' all the farmers woke up. Some of my audience even smiled.

I got into trouble for some of the things I did on my other varied visits . . . lowering the dignity of the office by playing football with the apprentices at Fairfields of Govan (the apprentices loved it), refereeing a football match at Elgin, or going out, in my robes, for a spin on the Blue Peter Inshore Rescue Boat, after launching it at North Berwick. In Glasgow the Lord Provost laid on an Ecumenical Lunch, with Nevile Davidson of Glasgow Cathedral, the Primus of the Scottish Episcopal Church, the Roman Catholic Archbishop, and even the Chief Rabbi. That afternoon when I came out of Ibrox after being entertained by Rangers FC, I was picketed by Jack Glass and his supporters with placards SMALL MUST GO (mercifully they did not say where), JOHN KNOX WOULD TURN IN HIS GRAVE (funny how we cannot get away from him).

Jack Glass missed out on my major iniquity. When Haddington and Dunbar Presbytery so happily came up in my rota, being my home Presbytery, I crashed through the sound barrier, and became the first Moderator since the Reformation to visit a Roman Catholic Abbey. I went to Nunraw to visit my old friend, the Abbot Columban Mulcahy. It was an historic occasion, fully covered by the press, both Catholic and Protestant. The dear man was so moved that his speech of welcome was almost inaudible. When the press asked for copies, he apologised that, while they had prepared them, knowing they would be wanted, they had put the carbon papers the wrong way in the typewriter. After showing me round, taking me to their noon service, and inviting me to pray for them there, we went for lunch . . . just the Abbot, the Prior, the Clerk and Moderator of Presbytery and myself. We got talking, first about Ian Paisley, about whom we were all agreed. Then they got on to Archie Craig's visit to Pope John, all these years ago.

Holy goalie, playing football with the apprentices at Fairfields' Shipyard, Govan

'Do you know how the two Church leaders said farewell?'

'No,' I replied.

'The Moderator said: "So long, John," and the Pope replied "A revederci, Erchie".'

To keep my end up I asked if they knew that the Pope had decided to let the Moderator out by the back of the Vatican, for fear of some demonstration. So they passed through the vast kitchen premises, passing a jolly-looking cleric, officiating at a pan of deep fat. 'I suppose,' said Archie, 'you'll be the principal frier?'

'No, Moderator,' he replied: 'I'm the Chipmunk.'

Finally, one of the brothers, slipping round on his sandal-shod feet, asked: 'Did you hear how the Holy Father greeted the Moderator? He just said: "Long time no Holy See"!' Nonsense, but happy nonsense, and how wonderful that we could be at ease like that, after the centuries of bitterness and often bigotry.

One other very special thing I did which, unexpectedly, got me into trouble, was the result of a promise made at my installation. My predecessor, Archie Watt, in reviewing his year, said he had been in every form of transport except a submarine! The Naval Officer commanding in Scotland, who was sitting in the Gallery, sent me a message, promising to make good this omission. As a result, on a wild and stormy day in February 1967, I was taken out on a tender, and made the awkward transfer to HM Submarine *Porpoise*, lying in Gourock Bay. She was not nuclear – one of the last of the big conventional boats, and she was suffering what in a car would be called a 'speed wobble' – at a certain depth and speed she developed a noisy vibration. There were 'boffins' from the Admiralty on board to try to trace and cure this. Owing to the stormy conditions the movement of the ship on the surface was violent and uncomfortable, but when we dived this was soon left behind. I remembered something I had read. Pastor Niemoller, a leading opponent of the Nazi regime, was kept for three years in solitary confinement in a tiny cell. When he was released, someone asked him how he had kept his sanity under such conditions. He replied: 'During World War I I was a U boat commander, and I discovered that no matter how stormy it was on the surface, ten fathoms down it was calm.' This I discovered with a thrill was true.

We went to the north of Arran, where there is a sort of trench in the bed of the Clyde 300' deep, where tests can be made at depth, which we proceeded to do. It was exciting to be asked to 'con' the submarine at that depth. I was shown all over, and was able to 'chat up' the crew, all of whom were volunteers for that kind of Service. I even dared to ask the captain if

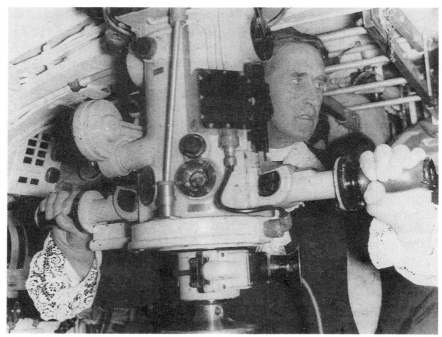

Conning HMS Porpoise, *submarine, at a depth of 50 fathoms*

they managed to carry out the Navy tradition, of holding Divine Service on a Sunday.

'Oh, yes!' he replied, 'We always do. We gather the off-duty men in the largest space we have. You'll be interested to know that the favourite Hymn is "Guide me, O thou great Jehovah".'

I like to think of the strains of Cwm Rhondda rising up from the depths, like the bubbles from a diver's helmet! The boffins decided that the Moderator must be a Jonah in reverse, for they found and corrected the fault by 4.00 p.m. and we were able to set off and dock at Faslane, which is where the trouble began.

A group of CND enthusiasts, led by one of my old Assistants, picketed me . . . 'This was the Moderator, in name of the Church, blessing nuclear warfare' . . . As I explained it was purely the fulfilling of a personal promise by the Naval Commander, and had nothing 'official' about it. Seeing it happened to be landing me at Faslane, the naval authorities had asked me, having been twelve years convener of a Committee dedicated to Forces Welfare, to look with them at the special welfare problems that were likely to arise when the entire crew of men were separated for at least six months from their wives and children, for security reasons totally 'incommunicado'. Just because we disapprove, on the surest grounds, of some action, does that mean that we should write off the human beings involved, as being somehow disqualified from receiving the Church's care?

The splendidly unique and unrepeatable item in my programme was the visit I paid for a month to all the Forces in the Far East, Malaysia, Singapore, and Hong Kong. Someone at the Ministry of Defence discovered that no Moderator, during his year of office, had ever paid such a visit – as they were all, sadly, withdrawn soon after, no one will do it again – it was very much a 'one off'.

My whole tour, involving, as it did, close cooperation between all three Services, was sponsored by the Royal Air Force, because of my long-standing connection with the Air Training Corps – I had been Chaplain to the Kilmarnock Squadron when the Corps was founded in February 1941 and, since 1953, Regional Chaplain for Scotland and Northern Ireland. They flew me from Lyneham in a Comet – a wonderful aircraft – and for the month I held the honorary rank of an Air Chief Marshal of the Royal Air Force! We were held up by engine trouble at Muharraq on the Persian Gulf, so fell hours behind schedule. As a result, instead of landing at Gan, in the Maldive Islands, almost on the equator, during darkness, we landed at midday. I came off the plane in the full moderatorial dress of heavy broadcloth, with no one else in more than a pair of shorts. I had left like that, in the cold of early March, but I should have explained that I had been instrumental in having established new official wear for a hot climate. I called the Moderator's Advisory Committee, and asked them to face the fact that, under modern conditions, every Moderator was going to spend some time in a hot climate. After some discussion it was agreed: a light-weight cassock, which could be worn over light underwear and two would allow for laundering each night – good, but what colour? Ronnie Falconer, BBC, suggested the light blue of the background of the St. Andrew's Cross flag. I got from Forsyth's a photostatic copy of the measurements of my normal black cassock, and air-mailed them to Sam Greer, the minister in Singapore. When I arrived, after Gan, I was presented with two beautifully tailored blue cassocks, plus a black one for evening wear, account £19.99 – made out to 'Rev. R.W. Forsyth, Ltd.'! The Chinese tailor had taken the heading off the Firm's paper!

There was an amusing personal touch early on. When I left home, our daughter Catriona was ten days overdue with her first child, sex not yet revealed. As we already had seven grandsons and no grand-daughters, I said to Jean: 'If it's another of those blooming boys, just cable me SOS, and I'll know it means "Still on sons".' Three days after my arrival I was at a very top brass dinner in the home of Sir Michael Carver, C. in C. Far East, Lord Mountbatten's successor. I was sitting between Lady Rockford Hughes, wife of the Air Officer Commanding, and Lady Twiss, wife of the Naval Officer Commanding – it was of that level. In the middle of the meal the Chief Steward tiptoed up and whispered:

'Could you come to the phone, sir? There's a cable been delivered to the Presbyterian Manse, and the minister is worried – it sounds like an emergency, that you would have to go home, when you've just arrived.'

Sam Greer read out: 'SOS both well. Love. Jean.'

'Does it mean you have to go home?'

'No, no! It just means it's yet another of those blooming boys.'

Then I had to go back and explain to my table of top brass. It paid off, for I got a gift for the baby from many of the Stations I visited.

Very early on I was taken to visit the great War Cemetery at KaiTak – nothing impressed me more – those rows upon rows of white stones with their varied inscriptions, so many Royal Scots, so many young, all too many with neither name, rank, nor number, just 'Known Unto God' – there they were, fallen in, row upon row, perfectly covered off, formed up, leading down to the sea, like some disciplined, orderly army, waiting to embark on a new expedition – and what deeper, more triumphant reality could there be?

I visited every Army, Navy and RAF installation in Singapore, along with schools, hospitals, clubs, garrison churches. In one RAF Station there was a moving personal touch. When I was visiting Dumfries Infirmary the previous autumn, I had talked to an elderly, pretty ill patient, who told me he had a daughter married to a sergeant on an RAF Station in Singapore. That patient died in January. As soon as I arrived at the particular Station, the CO said: 'Oh! Moderator; I've got Sergeant Macmillan and his wife waiting, would you see them first?' What must it have meant to that daughter, for I was the last person to have seen her father alive? I landed on the top of Penang Island, and viewed the main control centre for communications; I went out on a jungle exercise with the Commonwealth Brigade in the Malaysian Jungle in an area supposed to be infested with communist guerillas, Gurkhas playing with great glee the part of the

Hi-jacked in a tri-shaw, Singapore. The old man misunderstood his instructions!

guerillas; I took part in the Ordination of an elder whose District equalled in area all three Lothians put together. I flew in eight helicopters.

One in particular I remember. On Palm Sunday morning I was waiting at the heliport on the front at Hong Kong – I had moved there for a week – waiting for a helicopter which was to pick me up at 10.30 and take me to a Service at Sek Kong in the New Territories for 11.00. 10.35 – no helicopter. At 10.40 a little two-seater Scout whirly-bird came in and landed, and out stepped a young officer in tartan trews (he came from Locharbriggs near Dumfries). His opening gambit: 'I'm sorry, Moderator, but I couldn't get this blooming thing to start,' – how encouraging can you be? I can tell you I lifted that helicopter over the range of hills we had to surmount, the way I lift the horse over the high wall at Olympia. He did just 'get me to the Church on time'; the minute we landed I jumped out, ran in the back door, and climbed into the pulpit as the Choir finished the Introit.

That same afternoon I was taken to the top of Crest Hill (so called because when the Scots Guards were stationed there, they carved their crest in the turf of the hillside). There I looked over into Red China, the young soldier-guard's telescope focused on the gable of a public building with a large painting of Mao Tse Tung – the face which then, for about a quarter of the human race, took the place of the face of God. That same evening in the City Hall we listened to a marvellous performance of *Messiah*, with a chorus of 150, half of them Chinese. I shall never forget listening to that Chinese soprano, with a lovely voice, singing 'I know that my redeemer liveth' or the uplifting assurance of the Hallelujah Chorus: 'The kingdoms of this world are become the Kingdom of our God, and of His Christ' . . . that, with Red China just over the Border.

On a lighter vein, I inevitably went shopping. Margaret, Ken's wife, mentioned earlier, had been given instructions by Jean, and conducted me. This is an excellent safeguard, for a local trader will not cheat or overcharge you if escorted by a resident. She took me to a shop which had just a door and one window, but went deep to back shop and cellar. I asked him if he could produce any of those gorgeous embroidered silk kimonos, and could he give me five all different, for my wife, daughter, and three daughters-in-law? He asked, as a purely practical consideration: 'Do the ladies wear long nighties or shortie nighties?' I had to reply that there was only one of the five I saw regularly in her nightie, another not since she was about ten, the others never. 'Well,' he said, 'we settle for knee length,' and produced the goods, so lovely that all five of the delighted recipients used them as dresses!

Looking back on the varied experiences of that month, spent in these circumstances, in that area of costly errors in strategy, sinful muddle, horrible cruelty and ennobling sacrifice, I remember most the famous Changi murals, painted by one of the many prisoners in the notorious Changi Jail. They had recently traced the original artist, and got him to come and touch them up. The one that stands out in my memory most clearly shows Jesus laid on His back on the ground, on top of the Cross, while they hold His hands against it and nail Him to it, and He prays: 'Father, forgive them, for they know not what they do.'

Two other overseas visits must be mentioned. I went to Lisbon for the Centenary of the Scots Kirk, which was a great affair. In the more relaxed ecumenical climate, things happened that could never have happened before. In the packed Church about one quarter of the Congregation had never been at a Protestant Service before. Eight denominations were represented. The British and American ambassadors were present, and the

South African ambassador was ordained as an elder the following Sunday. Scots Kirks like that are great rallying centres for members of the Reformed faith from all over the world, and maintain a most important witness in these predominantly Roman Catholic countries. That same Scots Kirk gave shelter soon after to some fifty stranded Celtic supporters, who had been watching Celtic winning the European Cup! We had been supposed to go on to Gibraltar for a few days, but Franco was being difficult about the border, and it was decided not to risk it. For the days thus spare the British ambassador very kindly lent us his car and chauffeur, so we were able to do some luxury sightseeing. We held a meeting of the Presbytery of Western Europe, with three elders, including one from Gib., myself co-opted to make up a quorum, along with the Lisbon minister, and proceeded to appoint commissioners to the General Assembly! Seeing I had just come from visiting Glasgow Presbytery, the largest in the world, it was an interesting contrast.

Very near the end of my year I went to Hungary for the 400th Anniversary of the founding of the Hungarian Reformed Church, when that Church adhered to the Helvetic Confession of Faith. It was a strange experience . . . we could go where we liked, but were not allowed to stay overnight in a Hungarian household. The hotel arrangements were pretty chaotic; I ended up sharing a long, narrow room with the Irish Moderator. The celebrations were held in a great Church at Debrecen, about 200 kilometres east of Budapest, packed with about 5,000 people. The pulpit was like an opera box, sticking out high up on one long wall; from there you had to address the crowd. My address had been sent to Bertalan Tamas, Pastor of our Scottish Mission in Budapest, a fortnight before, not just to be translated but to be censored. I had taken up the fact that when the iron bridge over the Danube was being built, the Scots engineering firm sent out not only their erectors and engineers, but a Minister as Chaplain . . . hence our Kirk's continuing presence. I suggested that it would be a good idea to start rebuilding bridges between our countries, and mentioned that there had always been a Hungarian student at New College . . . that was censored out. I was allowed to leave in a reference to Miss Jane Haining, matron of a school for girls, who chose to go with her pupils and perished in Auschwitz Camp. It was a queer feeling, addressing that great crowd, and knowing that police spies were taking down and checking every word. I had to be got back to Budapest that evening in order to catch an early plane next morning to get home for our own Assembly. I was driven by one of their pastors, who took me in the evening to one of those restaurants where they play the zigane right under your nose. He got rather mellow, and from his wallet showed me with an air of secrecy, the credentials of a card-carrying member of the Communist Party. He explained that he was, in fact, the Associate Minister of one of their large Congregations, just 8,000 members. Knowing this, the local Party still wanted him to represent their Ward of the City, but he must have a card!

One final word, apropos of the much-criticised Moderatorial dress, which I wore with pride, without embarrassment, and found both 'kenspeckle' and comfortable. On the way home from Hungary, I was standing in Heathrow, studying the shuttle departure board, when I got a wallop between the shoulder blades. I turned round, to be confronted by a BA baggage man, who apologised when he saw my collar: 'I'm sorry, sir. I just wanted to say you've got the most "with it" rig-out I've seen for a long time!'

Chapter 14

The Parole Board

In the end of 1967, shortly after I had demitted office, Willie Ross, the Secretary of State for Scotland, asked me to become the first Chairman of the newly-formed Parole Board for Scotland. I think he wanted someone who would be reasonably well-known to the people of Scotland, as the immediate past Moderator tended to be, and, hopefully, would be trusted by them. I had long experience, since the Cramond days, as a member of the Scottish Advisory Committee on the Treatment of Offenders. I made it plain that I could do it only if it did not clash with any of my Parish duties. I had always felt that the Minister of a great City Church like St. Cuthbert's should play some part in the wider service of the Community, so I agreed to undertake this daunting responsibility, serving for three years, and then allowing myself to be persuaded into doing a second term. It was very interesting working with penologists, psychiatrists, chief constables, sheriffs and other professionals. I was very fortunate in having, as Vice-Chairman, that great man, Father Anthony Ross.

The principle we were committed to work out was that anyone who had committed an offence serious enough to attract a sentence of over eighteen months would normally, after scrutiny by a local committee, come up for consideration for parole, at one-third sentence. This was an extension of the prevailing system whereby, given good conduct in prison, the offender would be released at two-thirds sentence. This involved careful study of a variety of reports covering the nature of the crime and all the circumstances in which it was committed: the attitude to the offence – regret, remorse, even repentance, or none of these; behaviour and reaction to treatment in prison; advantage taken of training available – all these were 'background' information. Equally important was the situation to which the offender would go if released – home and family circumstances, prospects of employment, if any; supportive factors – or their opposite. As the system was new, and needed to earn the confidence of the public, we were very careful, perhaps ultra careful.

As time went on it began to emerge that the system could be made to work, indeed was working. We had an encouraging success rate, but problems emerged. One was the inadequacy of the training facilities available, coupled with the reluctance of the trade unions to accept at their full value any qualifications gained in prison. A young offender might do a painting and decorating course up to City and Guilds Certificate standard. On 'civvy street' he could only be employed as a brush hand. The media had an unhappy knack of highlighting only our failures, the more dramatic the better. Our one outstanding failure was a young man whose original offence was the murder of a night watchman, in an attempt to steal wages. Because it was murder in pursuit of gain he faced the death sentence, but because of his youth it was commuted to life imprisonment. He had served some twelve years, done well all through, and on Training for Freedom. The Board unanimously insisted that he be released on parole. Having no real home, he went, for fellowship, to the pub, got 'roarin' fu', got into a fight and killed a man. Over the six years, studying case histories like his, almost an inch thick, one came to know the depth of evil in human life, and the hideous things people can do to others, and themselves. I came to agree totally with the verdict: 'No civilisation, no political system, no philosophy of life can survive that does not take seriously the power of evil in human life.'

I came to the conclusion that many people enter into and get sunk in a life of crime because of the background from which they have come, and the downward drag of the setting to which they must return. Very many turn to crime because they are just inadequate . . . they are not even clever enough not to get caught! But we must not gloss over the fact that there is such a thing as a bad man or boy, woman or girl. Keeping it a simple level, a famous criminologist once said: 'We must recognise that a boy will steal cigarettes because he wants to smoke, and not because someone hit his mother over the head with a cigarbox three months before he was born!'

Drink, beyond all question, in one form or another, and in one way or another, plays a large part in serious crime. I ventured to speak about this in the General Assembly, recording my strong impression that there was a drink element in 60% of serious crime. When I came out I was accosted in the corridor by a tall, impressive-looking commissioner, with 'retired police inspector' written all over him.

'I want to take you up over what you've just said about drink being involved in 60% of crime. In my experience it is nearer 90%!'

There are some crimes that are so bizarre and hideous that you wonder why they do it. Early on we had the agonising case of a young woman of twenty-nine who murdered her small daughters, aged five and three, by putting polythene bags over their heads, and holding them till they suffocated. It was such an incredible crime that we searched back and back through her history for some possible causation. Eventually we discovered that when she herself was five her mother committed suicide, in a particularly horrible fashion, and in the child's presence. When she became a mother, that picture, burned on her memory, so haunted her with the fear of becoming that kind of mother, that she decided her children would be safer dead. She was released on condition that she did not marry and again have children.

Looking back, what shocks me most is not the brutal murders, but the meaningless violence, mostly by youth. A group of them knocked on the car window of a young husband, waiting to take his wife out for the evening. He turned it down, they slashed his face with a razor, and he was taken into hospital with his nose hanging on by a piece of gristle . . . a total stranger. One cannot help asking: 'My God, why?' My duties took me into all the prisons in Scotland, a grim experience. Quite outstanding in memory was the visit to the Special Unit, recently set up in Barlinnie. You had to pinch yourself to realise you were sitting having afternoon tea with five of the most dangerous criminals in Scotland. This was the time when Jimmy Boyle had developed his amazing gift for sculpture, and had a life-size head of Anthony Ross, which was a 'speaking likeness'. When we got into the official car to go back to Edinburgh, Anthony sat in the back seat, holding this sculptured head on his lap, covered in gilt (no pun implied!). I wickedly turned round and said: 'Anthony, I never thought I would live to see a Roman Catholic priest given his head in his hands to play with!'

I ended my spell of responsibility, greatly concerned about the inadequacy of our treatment of offenders, the grim, gratuitous ugliness of our prisons, the lack of positive training facilities, and the desperate inadequacy of support and supervision on release. When Father Ross and I visited the English Parole Board their members were rather mystified by the two clerical collars. I said to Lord Hunt, the Chairman: 'We are not here representing the main crime-producing sections of the Scottish population; we are here because we both believe, as servants of Christ, in the 3 Rs – Retribution, Renewal, Rehabilitation.' Looking back, to these I would cling.

Mention of Lord Hunt enables me to remark that one of the benefits of six years in that responsible position gave me the chance to know him as my opposite number. As it happened, I had met him and knew him already. In 1963 a great Boys' Brigade International Camp was held in the grounds of Trinity College, Glenalmond, when Sir John Hunt (as he then was) was Camp Commandant and I was Chief Chaplain – there were over 3,000 officers and boys from thirty-three different countries. Sir John gave the 'keynote' address in the huge marquee on the opening evening. I have never heard a more straightforward, Christ-centred talk to youth. He had an extraordinary influence on them. He just wandered around the camp, looking in at the widely varied activities – whatever they were doing they did better because he was watching them. The Staff were sleeping in Icelandic tents just in front of the School buildings. Although it was the first week of August, the first night was bitterly cold. At breakfast we were all moaning about the rigours we had been called upon to endure. A thought suddenly struck me and I said:

'Sir John, you must think we are all daft, when you remember what you endured on Everest.'

'On the contrary,' he replied, 'On Everest I found that any fool can be unnecessarily miserable – you only make yourself a liability to the rest of the team. If it's of any interest to the rest of you, I'm going into Crieff this morning to buy a hot-water bottle!'

We met on several occasions to decide upon a joint policy in connection with Parole, or to agree to back a parallel request to the powers that be. On one occasion, after having had a long talk in the George Hotel, we were standing outside, and I said:

'John, where are you making for?'

'Oh,' he said, 'I'm staying with a friend at Duddingston.'

Intending to offer a lift I asked: 'How are you thinking of getting there?'

'I'm going to walk,' said John.

I was about to retort: 'But you can't walk from the George to Duddingston,' when I remembered in time I was talking to a man who had climbed to the South Col of Everest. It was a rare privilege for a parish minister to get to know a man of that calibre.

I demitted office in the end of 1973, and next year was awarded the CBE 'For Public Services in Scotland'. This meant going down to Buckingham Palace for the Investiture, and I took Jean and Catriona with me. We had all three been before, for I had been awarded the OBE for services as Regional Chaplain to the Air Training Corps. The two visits had two things in common: first, Catriona had little concern for her father – the first time she was more interested in Stirling Moss, the racing driver, and the second

Outside Buckingham Palace after receiving the CBE. With Jean and Catriona

time, poor old Charlie Chaplin was being knighted! The second common denominator was that both times Jean remarked, without in any sense complaining, that you didn't even get a cup of coffee. The CBE occasion was special, because when my turn came, the Queen flashed one of her special smiles, and said: 'How nice to see you again, Dr Small. It is a great personal pleasure for me to give you this award.' When she said 'again' she meant the weekend I spent at Balmoral, just months before, when I sat beside her in the Land Rover, while she drove with great skill through the ruts and potholes of the rough road from Loch Muick to the Castle. That gives me the opportunity for referring, however briefly, to sundry contacts with the Royal Family.

Chapter 15

Contacts with 'The Royals'

There are three ways in which a minister can get himself invited to Balmoral. On the first Sunday of the Royal holiday the Minister of Crathie, the Queen's Domestic Chaplain, conducts the Service; on the second the Moderator stays the weekend and preaches; on each of the remaining Sundays the Guest Preacher is chosen by the Queen from a list of suggestions submitted by the Dean of the Chapel Royal. Her Majesty herself makes the final choice; on occasion she adds suggestions of her own. For example, on one occasion she remarked that the Church of Scotland organised several Chaplains to Industry; could someone come and talk to her about that – so George Wilkie went. It was under these auspices that I went for the first time, when we were in Cramond, very early in the Queen's reign. The invitation is from 5.00 p.m. on Saturday to 10.00 a.m. on Monday – so no one will be dumb enough to outstay their welcome! I went in fear and trembling, but it was all made very easy. I was 'genned up' over a cup of tea in the equerry's room, by a delightful lady-in-waiting, Lady Susan Hussey, a mother of a young family – she remarked how considerate the Queen was in not allowing young mothers like her to do long spells of duty away from the family.

My visit was made much simpler, as on future occasions, because there were no other guests, and the Royals were enjoying the chance to be just themselves. At dinner the Queen put me, sitting on her right, very much at my ease, by asking me if I was enjoying a made-up dish served in a large shell. When I replied that it was delicious, she said: 'I'm glad. I got the recipe from Woman's Hour on the radio.' After dinner we watched the film *The Caine Mutiny* in the ballroom. After lunch on Sunday afternoon, I went to the Manse for tea, then after dinner we played Scrabble. Some time over the weekend I asked the Queen if there was any truth in the American rumour that she was planning to give up the Balmoral holiday.

120

'Certainly not,' she replied, 'This is the only place on earth we can just be ourselves. When it comes to the last week I would do anything rather than go back to it all.' Then she added, mainly to herself: 'When I feel like that, I try to remind myself that everything that has happened to me, especially the Coronation Service, has proved that God will always give me the strength I need when I need it.' Over the passing years I have often remembered these words.

The next time I was there was in August 1966 as Moderator – the second way of getting yourself invited. There was a slight upgrading of status, from a single room on the first floor, to a suite on the ground floor. The overall pattern was the same; there were no other guests, but the family had been increased by the addition of Andrew and Edward. The highlight for me was that it was Anne's sixteenth birthday, and I sat beside her at all the meals. Andrew was observant enough to ask his father why the Minister had prayed for Anne today as he didn't usually get as far down the list as her. His father replied that he probably gave her a special mention because it was her birthday; if he prayed for her every Sunday, he would need to go right down the list and pray for little Edward – it would be an awful lot of people to pray for.

Anne herself was great fun. She had just finished her first session at Benenden School, so I asked her what she missed most through making the change.

'Oh, being in the Guides. I had only one test to do for my First Class – I'll never be a First Class Guide now.'

When I asked what she enjoyed most about being in the Guides, she said:

'Oh, going to camp – sleeping on the ground was super.'

Does anyone recall the fable about the princess, the thirty-two mattresses, and one hard green pea? She chatted away as any sixteen-year-old schoolgirl would. Then suddenly she blew her top and burst out:

'Oh, why do I have to be a princess? Why can't I be just me?'

It was so obviously a cry from the heart that it demanded some kind of answer. So, being old enough to be her grandfather, I said:

'Well, Anne, what matters is not who or what you are, but that, whatever you are, you should be your own best self.'

That, I would insist, she has done. Getting to Olympic standard as an equestrienne, figuring as Sportswoman of the Year, doing the work she has done for Save the Children, and now the support she gives to hosts of good causes. I never read the Court News in the *Scotsman* without noting that she seems to have three engagements every day. And that is not to mention the most important of them all – being the enthusiastic Patron of the Scottish Rugby XV!

I found myself that weekend advising the mother as well as the daughter. The Queen asked my advice regarding the relationship between the Crown and the Kirk, and the whole business of her appointing the Lord High Commissioner to the General Assembly. She felt that this was a most valuable, indeed unique, relationship; to keep it alive she felt every monarch, during his or her reign, should come in person at least once, otherwise the traditional phrase: 'We, being busy with our other weighty affairs are unable to attend in person etc.' would be seen as a mere formality. What would be the reactions if she came herself? 'General delight,' I at once replied. She had asked my predecessor, Archie Watt, and got the same answer. She went on to ask my successor, Roy Sanderson, with the same result. Then she came herself. She often discusses matters of Church and State with the Guest Preacher, for she herself says she knows the Ministers of the Church of Scotland better than the Clergy of the Church of England – in England she just gets to meet the bishops!

It was not all serious discussion – as usual a lighter mood was often struck. The set-up is that you say goodbye when the Queen goes off on Sunday night – they have breakfast in their own apartments. The Queen said goodbye very graciously, then turned back and said:

'Oh, Moderator, I nearly forgot to ask you if you have any connection with St. Cuthbert's Cooperative Society.'

I replied: 'No, ma'am; they pinched our name, but there's no connection.'

'You see,' she continued, 'Their coach-building department have repaired the Royal carriages; I knew you were the Minister of St. Cuthbert's, and just wondered if there was any connection.'

It was just pure, delightful mischief.

The third and final time I went to Balmoral, was by the third and only remaining method of getting invited. In 1967, after my year as Moderator, I was appointed one of Her Majesty's Chaplains in Scotland. The set-up is that the Royal Household in Scotland includes eight Chaplains, who are appointed by Her Majesty on the recommendation of the Dean of the Chapel Royal. At the age of seventy you are required to retire and return your parchment of appointment – thereafter, if Her Majesty chooses, you are reappointed an Extra Chaplain for the rest of your natural life. There are quite a lot of us in the latter category. The duties are purely honorary; you are entitled to wear the Royal red cassock at Services, and the purple stock with a suit. You are usually invited to Balmoral during your period as a member of the Household, which is why I went in 1973.

This was slightly different from previous occasions, less formal throughout. We began on the Saturday evening, not with dinner at the Castle, but with a barbecue supper at the shooting lodge at Loch Muick, where Queen Victoria stayed while the Castle was being built: it had recently been done up so that the dining room could be used by candlelight; the old range had been removed from the kitchen and replaced with a barbecue. It was the day of the Braemar Games, and everyone was in a relaxed mood. They were all amused by the report that an American had waded across the Dee, trying to get into the policies. He had come up out of the water, shaking himself like a spaniel, and climbed the bank, to be stopped by a London bobby who stepped out from behind a tree and said: 'It was a nice try, sir. Now just go back the way you came.' Back at the Castle, we were a small company; Philip and Anne were away at Kiev on equestrian business, but Charles was home after nearly a year on his frigate in the Caribbean. At Church on Sunday I preached a sermon on 'Holidays and Holy days', pointing out that in former times the only time ordinary people had a holiday was on a Saint's Day or other Holy Day, and pleading for the restoration in our era of strain and stress and noise and hurry of the idea of a holy day, a day that is different, offering not just recreation but re-creation. At lunch, after the ladies had left us, there was no one but Charles, the private secretary and myself. Charles said:

'Dr Small, can I ask you a question about the sermon?'

Wondering what was coming, I answered 'Yes, of course.'

'When you said we should have a Holy Day, did you mean we had to go to Church?'

'Not necessarily,' I replied, 'Going to Church is the normal, easily available way of having such a Holy Day, but it is not the only one. For instance, you could have a very helpful and effective Holy Day, all by yourself, on top of Lochnagar [the great mountain behind the castle].'

'I just wondered,' he replied, and there the subject was dropped.

In the afternoon I went to the Manse for tea, while the others went their several ways. At dinner the Queen said to Charles:

'Well, Charles, you came home on Friday; you fished the Dee on Saturday morning, and went to the Braemar Games in the afternoon; you went to the Kirk this morning; what did you do with yourself this afternoon?'

He gave me a funny look, and answered: 'I went up Lochnagar all by myself!'

Two very special occasions, one with the Queen Mother, the other with the Queen herself, came up ten years later, during my nine months as locum in St. Columba's, Pont Street, London, while the minister, Fraser

Greeting the Queen Mother to St. Columba's. Special Service for Music for Outdoor Blind

McLuskey, was off for his year as Moderator. Because of its special position in the life of the City St. Columba's often housed Special Services. One such was held fairly early on in my time there. It was the Annual Thanksgiving and Rededication Service for an organisation which provided Music for the Outdoor Blind, one of the innumerable such organisations of which HM The Queen Mother is Patron. Fraser McLuskey was their Chaplain and gave the address, while I took the Service. The last time I had foregathered with Her Majesty was in the shooting lodge at Loch Muick, when we had discussed grandchildren, and mutually agreed we got more fun out of them, than out of our children!

At the end of the Service she walked out the centre aisle with Fraser, and I was one step behind. She stopped at each pew, and shook hands three along on either side, which was as far as she could reach; if there was a guide dog, she clapped it. Coming close behind I saw the rapture on the faces of these blind people at being thus personally recognised. I was so moved that I went straight to the Church Secretary and dictated a letter to Her Majesty, describing what I had seen, and continuing:

To my personal knowledge, Your Majesty has been doing this kind of thing, and giving this quality of pleasure, for over fifty years. In 1928, when I was a student staying in the New College Settlement in the Pleasance, Your Majesty and your husband, then Duke and Duchess of York, came to visit the Settlement and the work being done. Two of us students went to the Longmore Hospital and collected a young woman patient, so crippled she was already in a wheel-chair. We got her safely settled at a corner where no one could stand in front of her. When the Royal visitors were walking slowly through the cheering crowds, you spotted this woman; you unobtrusively plucked at your husband's sleeve to attract his attention (no one but myself noticed); you both came over and spoke to that young crippled woman. She lived another fifty years, and always swore she was living off those few kind words. I feel that Your Majesty should know that, from what I saw that far-off day, to what I have described this very afternoon, there must be innumerable people forever indebted to your caring for the individual.

I got a charming letter from the Queen Mother's private secretary, saying how touched she was that anyone should so remember after all those years.

The other occasion, involving the Queen herself, was at the Centenary Service of St. Columba's, which I mention in the context, but will describe more fully here. The Service was celebrating the Centenary of the Church on the same site, and the timing of it produced a strange situation. Fraser was there as Moderator to convey the greetings of the General Assembly, so he could not also be the local Minister, and I had to welcome Her Majesty, then welcome him to his own Church! I was happy to function as one of Her Majesty's Chaplains in Scotland, and to remind her that, if you carry back her somewhat tangled line of Scots ancestry, you come to King Aidan, who was not crowned but ordained in Iona by Columba. I also got the chance, for which I had waited twenty-five years, to remind her of her visit to Iona. The papers at the time made much of the fact that she was the first living monarch to land there in six hundred years – the rest, forty-eight of them, kings of Scotland, Ireland, and Norway, came to be buried in the Reilig Oran. After Service in the Abbey the Royal party went back to *Britannia* and she sailed away west, then swung round and anchored in Loch na Keal in Mull, for the party to visit personal friends at Ulva Ferry. When they got ashore the Queen said to Philip: 'You take the children on ahead; I'll just sit and enjoy the sunshine, and catch you up later.' So there

Greeting the Queen to St. Columba's, Pont Street. Centenary of Church on that site

she sat, just a young woman in a tweed coat and skirt, brogue shoes, and a head square. In a few moments along came a couple of hikers, shook her excitedly by the shoulder, and exclaimed: 'Coo, you'll never guess who we've seen just up the road there – Philip and Charles and Anne, if you hurry up you can see them yourself!' They had no idea they were speaking to the Queen.

There is one further, most recent, contact, which may serve to round off these recollections. Three years ago I went to the Scout Service in St. George's Chapel, Windsor, having been awarded the Silver Acorn for service to Scouting. There was a great crowd, because the Queen was to inspect a Parade of Queen's Scouts in the great quadrangle of Windsor Castle. I was meekly queueing with the crowd, when an official came and hauled me out, saying there were places reserved for award winners, near the saluting base. I was pushed with the other latecomers, nowhere near the saluting base, but away in the left-hand corner of the quad. Just opposite our corner was a carved stone gateway, above whose arch was carved 'Sovereign's Gateway'. Just at that moment, the Queen, accompanied by the Chief Scout, came out of that same Gateway, turned left and proceeded to inspect this imposing parade of over a thousand Queen's Scouts. She took her time about it, chatting to this one and that, came to the disabled group, in the opposite corner to us, and spent a while with them. She was running out of time, so she went to the saluting base, took the salute, and when the Parade was over, walked off, ignoring all the 'smart Alecs' who had got near to be noticed. As she walked past our group (most of them Scots), she spotted me standing there, wearing my Queen's Chaplain purple stock and came over and shook hands. The Scots were all cock-a-hoop: 'She spoke to one of us and not the English!' – very naughty.

I have put together these personal contacts with four members of the Royal Family, the Queen herself, the Queen Mother, the Princess Royal and Prince Charles. That story of the Queen by the roadside in Mull, told me by the Commander of *Britannia*, reminds us that they are all human beings like ourselves, set in the fierce light of publicity. They all share, in varying ways, a sense of dedication to service, for the nation, for innumerable good causes, for people as individuals. They value the Balmoral holiday highly, for it enables them to get away, just to be themselves. Amid all the criticism I wish the public would realise how difficult and demanding a life it is. Having seen them as I describe, I have the greatest admiration for the way they stand up to it. Having been in America during the hoo-hah of a Primary for a Presidential Election, I am more than ever an unashamed Royalist. I am proud to wear the red cassock and purple stock of an extra Chaplain to the Queen.

Chapter 16

The Shadow on the Sun

I mentioned in the chapter on Australia the very trying experience we had when Jean was given the wrong treatment for her Parkinson's Disease – I have now come to the point when it all began, and it is time to put it in the context of its full thirteen years. The first public engagement for our Moderator, just after our own Assembly, is to attend the General Assembly of the Presbyterian Church in Ireland. You might say that at that point in our life together we had reached the summit of privilege and blessing, even of achievement. We had been thirty-five years married, had shared in the Ministry in four Congregations, had brought up four children, and decorated the front pew in the Moderator's Gallery with a daughter and three daughters-in-law, all 'easy on the eye', and my youngest son was my Junior Chaplain – all without any serious mishap, or period of illness, or other shadow falling across the sunshine of happiness and success. That was the precise moment when the edge of what was to become a shadow, dark indeed, began to creep across our sun. At that opening day of the Assembly in Belfast, Ian Paisley staged the first of his big riots, with about 3,000 people, a band every fifty yards, marching round and round the block in which the Assembly was being held, yelling their protests against the Irish Presbyterian Church being in the British Council of Churches. At the end of the Opening Ceremony, Jean, coming out of the VIP Gallery with Lady Erskine, wife of the Governor of Ireland, was pushed right out to the edge of the pavement, right into this yelling mob. Lady Erskine started a nervous breakdown, from which she never really recovered, and Jean started Parkinson's. This was the diagnosis of Professor Gillingham, when he studied her case-history, with a view to doing a brain operation. He was almost laughed at at the time, but is now fully vindicated. It is clearly established that violent, sharp shock is accepted as one of the causes that can trigger off this insidious disease.

The first I noticed, later in that busy year 1966–67, was her hand shaking, but just thought it was excitement or stress. When the real trouble was diagnosed, she was sent to a neurologist, who told her there was not much could be done, gave her a general tranquilliser, and more or less told her she had to live with it, which she proceeded to do. Then in 1969 Colin told me that Professor John Gillingham in the Western General Hospital was doing a brain operation that was proving successful. The Professor 'owed me one' because he had lived at Cramond and I had christened one of his sons. He kindly took over and, after careful assessment of her case, proceeded to carry out the operation. It had to be done under a local anaesthetic, so as to observe the patient's reactions. It meant, of course, having her head shaved, which was inevitably a source of feminine embarrassment, and was made into a source of fun. The family pointed out what an opportunity it was, with high-class wigs now available: 'Mum, you can be a Spanish brunette, a Titian red, or a glamorous blonde.' When I added: 'What about a blonde? Gentlemen prefer blondes,' the victim flashed back: 'You were never a gentleman!' In the end she settled for, and settled down to wear, something not too extreme. It was at the time when *The Magic Roundabout* was popular on children's TV, so Mum's wig was affectionately known as 'Dougal' from the Scots terrier in that famous programme! All that fun helped her to face up to what must have been a pretty traumatic experience. When she expatiated on what it was like to have your head numb and still hear them sawing through your skull, Colin asked: 'Mum, when they got through, did they find anything?' That sense of humour, which she fully shared, was to prove a saving grace from first to last. The Professor put an electric probe into her brain, checking and rechecking meticulously, because, as he told me, he had to be exact to the tenth part of a millimetre, then passed an electric charge through and burned out the dead cells. It was like a miracle – her hand stopped shaking as if a switch had been switched off, and for a year she was back to normal. Then the trouble started again on the other side of the brain, where the operation is not done for fear of destroying the power of speech. Fortunately, just about that time the new drugs like L dopa became available, and the operation became almost redundant. The drugs kept the symptons under control, and she was able to go to Melbourne in 1971 with little or no inhibitions.

While the symptons of Parkinson's Disease can be controlled by the new drugs its relentless onward move continues. Gradually Jean's disability increased. Many of its forms were frustrating, like being unable to sing a note – the woman whom Dame Patty Menzies thanked for her singing in St. Stephen's, Sydney; or having no strength to pull through the threads of her beloved tapestry, that utter weakness in the hands that stitched her marvellous tapestry of da Vinci's painting of 'The Last Supper', all its 81,000 stitches. Often it was embarrassing, like stumbling with little, short steps – the phenomenon known as 'festination' – or the messy difficulty of controlling the necessary process of eating and drinking, and latterly accepting the indignity of wearing a 'pelican bib'. I had been told to keep her going as long as possible, so we went for a walk as often we could, to begin with, up Craighouse Hill behind the house, with its lovely panorama of the City; when that became 'out of range' we would set out each evening, down Craiglea Drive, and up Comiston, or vice versa. She could manage only about a hundred yards, so we had all the low garden walls staked out for her to sit and rest – I still note them when I pass that way.

I have described fully in their context those traumatic months in Melbourne in 1976, when she was given the wrong drugs. After we came back, and she was re-stabilised on a revised dosage, she seemed to do better. I took her twice a week to the Day Hospital at the City Hospital where she got therapy. This lasted for two years. Then came that miraculous spell in 1979 when she managed to live so fully on that final 'bonus' visit to Australia. After we came home in the joy and wonder of that amazing experience, it was as if she said her Nunc Dimittis, for she gradually but steadily went downhill. She went into the City Hospital in the end of July, and was very carefully and kindly looked after. I had to accept, as many another before and since, that I was no longer able to provide the skilled and constant care she needed. We used to take her out with a fellow-patient around the Hospital for what we called The Wheel-Chair Derby! The weakness increased till she lay quietly with no response, but we still took in the tape recorder and played her favourites like 'Jesu, Joy of Man's Desiring' or 'Fingal's Cave Overture', and I am sure the music got through. Finally she died, just sleeping and not waking, on 26 October. I was profoundly glad to see her set free, for the tragedy of these degenerative diseases is that you are left with a grey, shrivelled travesty of the happy, vital, radiant person you have known. Yet even in dying she left a strange legacy of blessing, for I find that I can now help people in bereavement far better than before . . . there are deep experiences you can share only when you have been through them yourself.

In all those shadowed years, I don't think I ever asked: 'My God, why?' – I often asked: 'My God, how? How are we going to bear and share this, as we have done all else, in these forty-eight years of life together?' That prayer was always answered, for amazing grace did not fail either of us. Her funeral service, in Mortonhall Main Chapel, which, strangely, I had dedicated as Moderator in 1967, beautifully conducted by our Minister in Greenbank Church, Donald Mackay, was uplifting and full of the right note of thanksgiving, and as we as a family, children and the twelve grandchildren, moved towards the Cross, set like a great Plus Sign above the catafalque, I remembered then, as often since, the saying of Mary Webb, the novelist: 'Christ has made death to be no more than a gateway on the skyline of life.'

Chapter 17

Iona

Much earlier on I referred to my first visit to Iona for the students' retreat, and to our honeymoon in that lovely Island. All down the years our holidays in and love for Iona have continued, and that has applied most happily to our children and children's children. Our first time back was when Ronald was five months old. Mrs Kirk, a doctor's widow in our Bathgate congregation, had taken a house in the middle of the village, *Mho Dhaiichaid*, My Home, for the month of June, and was not well enough to go, so she kindly offered it to us. There was no hot water in the house, so early each evening I went down and brought up two pails of salt water, in which, duly heated, the baby was bathed. Not many infants have a beginning like that! Granny McGregor, Jean's mother, was with us; we borrowed an old-fashioned high pram, took out the bottom boards, put in the pans with mince and tatties, and all else needed for an all-day picnic, and set out for the North End, below the croft of Lagandoran. There we would spend a whole day, with the sun shining and the larks singing – quite lovely. When we had Colin added we stayed in a small croft, again near the North End, called *Cnoc-cul-Phaul*, The Hill of Paul, and went to the same place till it became known to us and the locals as 'Smalls' Corner'. When Jean came off the steamer *King George V*, with Alan in a carry-cot, John More, the blacksmith who ran the red boats that ferried us ashore, exclaimed: 'Och! here she comes with another of them.'

The few years before the War were memorable for some rare boat trips to other islands. Captain Mcleod, a retired master mariner of great experience, took us one day, first to the two small islands with strange fortifications, Cairnsburg Mhor and Cairnsburg Beg, then on to Staffa, with plenty of time to wander around, not just in the Cave, but on the grassy top, with its ruined houses; finally, for the rest of the day to Lunga, with the marvellous bird sanctuary on the far side, where a great stack of rock has broken away and provides a perfect sanctuary, with a great gulf, only yards wide, yet offering total invulnerability to every kind of seabird. It was on that same island that the famous naturalist Frank Fraser Darling and his wife and two children camped one summer later on – in that total isolation the children went down with scarlet fever – no one knows how they caught it! Then in 1938, the year before the War, there was an unprecedented long weekend of perfect calm.

On the Saturday Captain Mcleod took a party to Skerryvore, the great lighthouse tower, fifteen miles south-west of Tiree. We were able to tie up the *Staffa* in a sheltered gully, and step ashore on the rocks. Years later the lighthouse was burned out and the granite tower was cracked by the heat, funnelled upwards. It was repaired and still functions; it is still manned but will probably soon be made automatic. On the Monday we went to Dhu Heartach, eleven miles south-west of Iona, where it was not so easy. The tower stands on St. John's Rock, a plug rising straight out of the Atlantic,. It had initially to be built on Erraid, the tidal island off the corner of Mull, which was then the lighthouse base, and shore home for the keepers and their families. The stones were quarried, carefully numbered, erected, taken down and ferried out to the rock – there were only sixty-one days in the year they were able to work on the rock. It was a great engineering feat by the famous Stevenson firm, who built so many wonderful lighthouses. R.L.S. himself lived on Erraid while all of this was going on, and got some of the ideas, like the unnecessary marooning of David Balfour, when in *Kidnapped* he was washed ashore from the wreck – he could have waded ashore at low tide at the narrows. The bay where he landed is called Balfour's Bay, and is one of the loveliest spots on earth. Out at the rock, we still could not go alongside, but had to lie off. The keepers come to an iron pier, throw you a rope: you pull that out till you come to a breeches buoy, attached to a block and tackle, which they are controlling from above. The principle is that the person going ashore sits in the chair, the keepers hoist away, you keep strain against them until he is high enough, then gently let him swing in to the rock. We had with us Donald McCuish, the minister of Iona, for the rock is in the Parish. It was unanimously decided he must go ashore first. There he sat in the bo'sun's chair; the keepers hauled away; none of us knew the technique, so as soon as his feet were clear of the gunwale, we let him swing like a pendulum – of course he went right under till only his hat was showing! One marvelled at the life of those keepers, keeping that essential light burning. I asked what it was like in a storm. The head keeper replied: 'In a bad storm the wave, not the spray, washes against the kitchen window; you can feel her give; if she didn't give she would go.' Now, the rock stands

47' above high water, and the tower rises 147' above that, so you can imagine the size of the wave. That tower, too, is now being made automatic.

That same year, 1938, another, very special, building project was being started. I mean the rebuilding of the Abbey ruined monastic buildings, and the founding of the Iona Community. I had better, here and now, clarify my own position in relation to the Community, and to George MacLeod, its Founder. Almost everyone seemed to take it for granted that I would join the Community, but I never felt like doing it. I had been long enough in Iona, and closely enough involved in the islanders' life, to share their hurt, amounting to resentment, at the autocratic way in which George imposed his plans and ideas on them. They didn't take kindly to being told when and under what conditions they could have the use of the building they had come to regard as 'theirs'. I was associated, directly or indirectly, with the work of the Community from the beginning. The first hut, in which the early members lived and moved and had their being, was built at the easternmost edge of the Abbey precincts, under the supervision of James Bowman, teacher of technical subjects in Ayr Academy, who at the age of twenty-nine was my youngest ever Session Clerk in Kilmarnock, and one of his helpers was Leslie Dickie, a member of our YPF. On one famous occasion I gave most strenuous practical help. One morning the Community members unloaded from a barge on to the jetty twenty-five one-hundred weight bags of cement. Then they went off to have their lunch, forgetting about the rising tide. From our house in the village I watched the tide creeping up the jetty nearer and nearer to the destruction of that much-needed material; I could stand it no longer, went down to the jetty and humped those bags, by getting each balanced on my knees and crab-walking, high enough up to safety – all twenty-five of them. I still don't know how I did it; afterwards I had a sore back (no wonder) and sore knees, and the next time it rained and I got my kilt soaked it stood by itself, as stiff as a board with engrained cement!

Over the years I maintained that ambivalent attitude, not disapproving, anything but, yet never able to 'go the whole hog'. I don't think George knew quite what to make of me. Matters were not helped at the time of the prolonged controversy when George wanted to go back to Govan Old and remain Leader of the Community. By the time the Assembly refused to sanction such an arrangement *'jus devolutum'* had come into force – the Congregation had lost the right to call their own Minister, and must accept whomsoever the Presbytery might choose. Dr John White and Professor Riddell were empowered by the Presbytery to make this difficult choice and they asked me! We got the length of going to see the Govan situation and visited the Pearce Institute. Jean and I both felt that I would be a useless misfit. It was precisely at this time that George got engaged to Lorna. Packed with the crowd in Shuna in Iona, for the engagement party, Jean found herself wedged in a corner with George, and quite naturally and in all innocence said: 'Oh, George, Leonard's wanting to ask your advice. He's been asked to go to Govan!' This was the same woman who had once said to him that the best stage in his ministry was the period when he was in St. Cuthbert's, to which he had replied that he wasn't preaching the Gospel then. From my nineteen years' experience in St. Cuthbert's I feel there was a great deal to be said for my wife's contention. He exercised a tremendous influence, especially among the young professional men of the city, lawyers, accountants and the like. I feel very strongly that in all the tributes and biographical records this has been undervalued.

Soon after that engagement party in Iona, George and Lorna went off to Australia and New Zealand on a trip which was part honeymoon, part propaganda tour to raise interest in and support for the Iona Community. Our visit to Dunedin came soon after and we got a 'sough' of the impression he had left. Knox Church were so typically Scots that the only thing they remembered was that he was the only man ever took up three collections in one Service! There was a wonderful story filtered down from Auckland. George wanted some of the lovely New Zealand hardwoods to line the Michael Chapel from floor to floor, right over the curve of the roof. He always went for the biggest firm available. Enquiries were encouraging; the firm in that category had a name like Mactaggart and McKillop, or something equally promising; unfortunately the partner in charge of export was returning from America just as George was due to leave from Auckland Airport, so he practically met him on the tarmac. There was no time to 'soften him up'; he just had to say who he was, and what he wanted, and waited for the volley. The timber baron gave him a strange look, and said:

'I'll be delighted to give you as much timber as you want. You couldn't possibly know it, but you have given back to me today something I discarded fifty years ago. I was born in Kirkintilloch and served my time as a joiner. When my time was out, along with my pal, I was given a choice of doing one of two things, to emigrate to New Zealand and try to make fame and fortune, which, you notice, we have done; the other was to join the squad of tradesmen putting the roof on the restored Abbey of Iona!' If that's not being charismatic, I don't know what is.

After the War was over our holiday pattern reverted to normal. During these passing years two momentous events stand out. When the family was small, the best we could do to get a picnic off the island was to borrow a rowing dinghy from Neil Macarthur, *Clachanach*. This was a small wooden craft, not easy to row with picnic gear and family. We always went to the island off the North End, with a lovely spit of white sand. It was called Eilean Annaraidh, but wasn't pronounced anything like that. I always seemed to time it to row against the tide, both ways. Then a Cramond elder, Dick Scales, who was a trawler owner in Granton, gave the family a 17' boat, which had been used as a trawler's lifeboat, based on Oban during the War. She was lying at Kerrera, painted a 'gooey' green, had been used for fishing and was a proper mess. She had a metal centreboard, mast and sails, jib and dipping lug, and all sorts of extras, like rubber inflatable dinghies. She was called *Ranger* but was re-christened the *Tern* and over the years has been the object of much tender and loving care, with a new centreboard, new thwarts and 'elbows', and a most attractive colour scheme of blues and white. When the family came back from the South Carolina exchange, having been given £100 to buy a TV, they spent instead £48 on a long-shaft Seagull outboard motor, and £25 on an 8' punt to act as tender. The *Tern*

Mooring the Tern *at Iona jetty; Jean passing rope through ring; RLS in famous kilt*

has been the joy of our lives in two generations, enabling us to go all-day picnics to Balfour's Bay in Erraid, or Market Bay in Mull, where they used to land cattle raised in Tiree, rowed there in flat-bottomed boats, then staged further on by boat and road to Falkirk Tryst. Alan has even taken his family quite happily to Staffa on a reasonably calm day. In more recent years the proceeds of one of grandfather's trips to Australia have replaced the old Seagull with a powerful Yamaha and we have the back-up of a 10' fibreglass dinghy with a Johnson outboard.

The other, even more momentous, event was the acquiring of a house of our own. After the War we had been going for several years to Knock-na-cross, next door to the Argyll Hotel in the middle of the village street. It was a good solid house, with walls 2½' thick of Ross of Mull granite, built over a hundred years ago by one man, a mason from Tiree, who was paid £18 for building it! It was in poor condition, for old Katy McLean, who had inherited a 99-year lease, was too proud to take the pension. She had nothing but what she made from summer letting, and as she charged us £18.50 for August, including half a ton of coal, she didn't have much. There was a WC but no hot water and no bath and no electricity; in the middle of the month we took the bath from under one of the beds and put it, 3' in radius and about 9" deep, in front of the range, put on everything that would boil water and, starting with the smallest, worked up to the parents. The range was a heartbreak; the oven if working would cook or bake anything, but the flue control kept coming off the hook, and had to be manipulated when the handle was almost red hot. Worst of all, the bottom ribs of the fireplace were loose, and if you poked too violently the fire fell into the ashpan, and you had to start all over again. The alternative was two temperamental primus stoves. At the back, built on, was a two-room house, built of very solid corrugated iron, where Katy lived when we were in the main house. Attached were an earth closet and a coal cellar. Over the back door was a tiny scullery, with an earthenware sink with a worm-eaten draining board, and newspaper stuffed under the corrugated iron roof, or when it rained it was like being in a shower. However, it was the Iona holiday, and we managed to make do. The boys usually camped in the front garden; that way they could have some of their pals. Eventually in 1964 Katy died, the 99-year lease was up and the house reverted to the Duke of Argyll, who put it on the market. It just so happened that the insurance I had taken out with the money put in my infant hands so long ago, matured that same year so, only under pressure from the family, we were able to put in an offer and, to our chagrin, got the house.

We got a firm of builders from Oban to renew the roof; Angy Mackay, former ship's carpenter, from Highland Cottage, next door but one, put in the new windows we sent up, so the house was now wind- and water-tight. During the winter Angy built on at the back, replacing the old scullery, a kitchen cum dining room, for which he charged us £150! We supplied the materials not locally available. Getting the furniture up to Iona was a problem. We could furnish completely with what we had collected in the top storey of the Manse, but all the estimates were prohibitive. Then our neighbours next door offered us acres of underfelting which they had replaced by rubber-backed carpets; we wrapped each item like a parcel in the underfelt; a small removal firm took it all up to the south pier, Oban, for £58, and Alistair Gibson, the Iona ferryman, took it all round to Iona in his fishing boat for £25! I must remark that, although the date was 9 July, we were storm-stayed at Fionnphort for two days, as was the fishing boat with the furniture. The next summer we had a marvellous week . . . I had bought from the Grassmarket a brick fireplace which came in three sections. We borrowed an old, sturdy Morris Traveller, got the fireplace stowed in the back, drove up and arrived at Fionnphort at the same time as the plumber and his mates from Tobermory who helped to load it on the ferry boat. All that week we were in the house with three plumbers, two electricians, and Angy 'making good'; they took out the old range, fitted the brick fireplace, with a Baxi to heat the water, put in a bath, handbasin, toilet, entire water system, wired for power and light, and we went home on Saturday. Since then we have had a steady programme of improvement and Knock-na-cross must be one of the best equipped houses in Iona. We also did up the backhouse. It now has a room with four bunk beds for the boys, and the girls' room with three beds. We also built on a workshop, and coal cellar, and finally a boat shed large enough to house the *Tern* and Colin's sailing dinghy, the *Seona*. Every beam and piece of timber in that complex of buildings came from the sea, the fruits of our many beach-combing expeditions, including the main beam across the front of the boathouse, 15' x 9" x 4". The sea which yielded up this harvest is not always kindly. I have hinted at the many occasions when we were storm-stayed, the Sound a mass of breaking seas.

There was one tragic weekend, after a Saturday night of threatening calm. A lovely old-fashioned yacht, the *Vala*, anchored overnight in Martyrs' Bay just south of the jetty. The man in charge came ashore on Sunday morning to get stores, a fierce storm sprang up from the south; he could not get back, and we had to stand and watch that lovely boat smash to pieces, the wreckage strewn all along the village beaches. During that same storm that lasted for days, one of the red boats that ferried passengers, fifty at a time, to and from the steamer, was driven high up on Rocky Island at the north side of the bay. The men on board jumped onto the rock and tried to fend her off by putting bottom boards under her bilges, with the waves breaking right over them; along with the men was Ronald who had been helping to crew and Colin was in the other boat, lying off waiting to help . . . talk about anxious parents! The situation was saved by a brave boatman rowing across with a line which made contact, and enabled the other red boat, as the tide rose, to tow the stranded one to safety. We at once claimed the boys and hurried them to where a hot bath had been arranged. They had been wearing those olive green anti-gas outfits which were then popular, with elastic at the cuffs and ankles and, having been on that rock with the waves breaking over them, or on the other one, similarly wave-swept, they were hardly damp underneath!

In all these sixty years of going regularly to Iona, I, and my family, had always been involved in the normal Island life – I had run in a relay race, and played football (holy goalie again) for the Island – they seemed to regard me as a sort of 'adopted' Islander. When I was Moderator they presented me with a pair of beautiful Celtic silver clasps for my cloak, designed and made by Ian McCormick, who was a teacher of technical subjects in Paisley. When the Presbytery decided to move the resident Parish Minister from Iona to Bunessan, five miles away on Mull, the Kirk Session appealed to the General Assembly, and I spoke out strongly on their behalf, citing Iona's long history and worldwide influence, and ending by declaring that 'for a Church that calls itself the National Church to have no resident Parish Minister in Iona is a national disgrace.' I was rudely told by the Presbytery Clerk that I was talking sentimental nonsense, that all that mattered was saving money and manpower. In the end they did neither. When they went on to stop dead the gallant effort of the Islanders to send out an appeal and carry out a bold scheme to restore the Manse and Church and create a Heritage Centre, the Kirk Session again appealed to the Assembly. This time I persuaded the Assembly to take the 'disposal' of the Manse completely from the Presbytery, and remit it with powers to the General Trustees. They sent a sub-committee to meet the Islanders, and were so impressed that they gave them *carte blanche* to go on with the whole scheme, which they have done successfully. They kindly asked me, having fought their battles for them, to open the Centre, which I did two years ago. So, having begun this tale by talking of a sense of Heritage, one of my last public functions has been to open a Heritage Centre!

Chapter 18

Retirement

I retired on 30 September 1975, having attained the age of seventy, and kept my promise to St. Cuthbert's to stay till then, to delay as long as possible the lapsing of the special Act of the General Assembly governing the situation for the duration of my Ministry. Thanks to the new relaxations in regard to vacancies, I was able to intimate my intention as early as December 1974. In view of Jean's disability I got permission to move at that earlier date to our retirement house, at The Moorings, at the back of Craighouse Hill, with a fine view of the backcloth of the Pentlands. We had bought it a few years before from Colin, when he was moving to a bigger house, and had let it furnished, mainly to a succession of doctors doing a year's post-graduate study. This early move proved to be just as well, as it took us the whole nine months to clear out the Manse!

We had a marvellous send-off, with a meal in the Main Hall, old friends from all our former Congregations, and a representative group of distinguished speakers. The 'menu' was as follows:

'The Communicator' . . . The Rev. Ronald Falconer, BBC (radio and TV).

'The Parole Board' . . . The Very Rev. Father Anthony Ross, Vice-Chairman.

'The West End Churches' . . . The Rev. Canon Aeneas Mackintosh, Rector, St. John's.

'The Fellow Minister' . . . The Very Rev. Dr David Steel (Former interim-Associate).

'The Moderator' . . . The Right Rev. Dr James G. Matheson, Moderator.

'The Minister's Wife' . . . Ian T. Campbell, Elder.

'The Minister' . . . Mrs Annis Frackleton, Elder.

Jean insisted on making a short speech of thanks for her gift, and 'brought the house down'. The whole proceedings were meticulously planned, and splendidly chaired by Douglas Grant, whose father, though a member of a City Church, used to be a regular attender at Cramond Kirk.

For good measure, Gordon Powell, formerly of St. Stephen's, Sydney, and Scots Kirk, Melbourne, now moved to Christ Church on Quaker Hill, Pawling, New York, sent a letter from which I quote:

> We owe a great debt to St. Cuthbert's for releasing him for these lengthy overseas visits. At the same time untold thousands of Australians had their lives spiritually enriched by his ministries in our country. One day, I hope, a book will be written about Dr Small's total ministry. If it is, several chapters will need to be devoted to what God did through him in Australia and New Zealand. We also thank God for the visits of Mrs Small, and her own special ministry.

Since this purports to be the book he refers to, I have ventured to include this quote from his letter.

For my farewell News Letter to the Congregation my indefatigable Secretary, Moira Currie, managed to 'winkle out' some statistics, revealing something of what it meant, as sole Minister of St. Cuthbert's (the first such since the Reformation) to try to be pastor as well as preacher. In those nineteen years I baptised 884 babies, visiting the families beforehand; confirmed 1,126 First Communicants, meeting with them in the Class and interviewing them privately in the Manse; celebrated 751 weddings, involving arrangements and rehearsals before and quite often the reception afterwards; ordained or admitted 132 elders, involving at least two or three visits to discuss the tasks of the eldership; and finally, conducted approximately 1,200 funerals, with the close personal contacts these sad occasions involve. When you add to all that the regular visits to members in hospital, which I always made a priority, this constitutes a wealth of personal involvement. Looking back now, this is what I value most, and for this I am deeply grateful.

The next year, as already described, we went for the five months to Australia, which turned out to be such a traumatic experience. After coming back it took some time to recover. From then on we were 'ticking over', being limited by Jean's increasing disability. I spent some time drawing on my Kirkcudbright great-grandfather's skills, and built on at the back of the house a sun lounge, 12' x 9', built of breeze blocks and cedar. I even drew the plans myself, allowing for a 5' fall of the ground, and got them through the Dean of Guild Court without question. In the course of laying the foundations a gang of grandsons barrowed, shovelled, laid and levelled four tons of cement from a mobile mixer in three hours, at 50 pence a time! It made a splendid place for Jean to sit, when she could do little else. I also spent an interesting year as Moderator of the Edinburgh Presbytery, never having been available before. Came the end of 1978, the appeal for help in an emergency from Scots, Melbourne, and that miraculous final visit. After our return in May 1979 came the accelerated decline in Jean's condition, her hospitalisation, and death, finally, on 26 October. It had an air of finality; it was the end of a life, not just hers as an individual, but the forty-eight years of wonderful shared experience; there was nothing to look forward to but the difficult adjustment to a life that must be totally different. By the grace of God my life thereafter worked out amazingly. So I now come to what I can only call 'The Bonus Years'.

Chapter 19

The Bonus Years

It took me many months to readjust after Jean's death; for at least the last five years her care had been my inescapable concern, waking and sleeping, and for long enough your hands feel empty, as every carer too well knows. Then in the summer of 1980, I accepted the invitation to go to Toronto for the Ordination of Joan Mackintosh, a Canadian girl who had come to St. Cuthbert's when she was training in the Royal Infirmary. It was an interesting experience. The United Church carried out Ordinations differently from us – we ordain in the Church where the Minister is to serve – they ordained together all who had finished their Course, twenty-nine in all. The Service was held in Barrie, a town about a hundred miles north of Toronto, and in a beautiful new RC Church, the only one big enough. It was a most impressive Service – all twenty-nine took their vows together, then came forward, one at a time and knelt at a prayer desk; behind it stood the President, Clerk and Convener of Students of the Toronto Conference. On either side of the kneeling candidate stood a sponsor. One such sponsor stuck out like a sore thumb; she was dressed in patched and ragged denims, with a blouse none too clean, her hair in a pony tail, tied with a shoe-lace, her feet bare and not clean either – she was a feminist registering her protest, which seemed to me ill timed and insulting.

Joan had arranged for me to preach in three Toronto Churches, including the incredibly wealthy Timothy Eaton Memorial. I found Toronto a lovely and wonderfully clean city, with an efficient and spotless Underground. I also preached for Joan in her own congregation at Mount Forest, among the dairy farmers, mostly from Northern Ireland and nowhere near the bread line! From there I flew to Victoria, BC, to stay with a couple I had married in Cramond thirty-three years before. They took me to see the woman who ran their local Post Office. She turned out to be Susan Greenshields, daughter of our Sunday School Superintendent in

Kilmarnock, and a young mother showed me a wonderful dolls' house she had brought out because I had shown it in the pulpit in the same Kirk. My beach-combing soul still shudders at the dreadful waste of the huge logs strewing the beaches, broken off the log-rafts. From there I flew to Edmonton to stay with Ron and Fiona Fraser – Ron was a fellow-student and pal of Colin, now a busy surgeon. They took me to Jasper to see the Rockies, which was a wonderful experience, enhanced because I had flown over them on the way to Victoria. It was there I blotted my copy-book. After a tiring day we went to some splendid sulphur springs discovered by the Red Indians – wonderfully relaxing, and so warm you were advised not to stay in more than twenty-five minutes. After twenty I had had enough, climbed out and, as I thought, retraced my steps, only to find myself in the ladies' dressing-room (with nobody in). Ron had excused me by announcing that I was a stranger from Scotland, whereupon I defied them all by declaring loudly that it was their own fault for putting on the door that cut-out of a man in a kilt!

From there I flew back to Toronto, then down to South Carolina once again. On that last flight I had an interesting companion, a tall, military-looking gentleman who, sensing that I came from Britain, asked if I had watched the TV series on Colditz. When I said I had he remarked that it was not as easy as it was made out to be, because Pat Reid, who wrote the series, escaped after only one year.

'I', he went on, 'was there for three years; when I escaped I walked all the way to Switzerland, keeping alive by digging up the seed potatoes and eating them. I'll give you three guesses what I do now.'

I replied that he projected the image of a big business tycoon.

'That's only what I do for a living; I'm a member of Billy Graham's Gospel Choir!' One meets strange folk.

Next year a succession of events took over. I went out to St. Stephen's, Sydney, to act as locum, while Graham Hardy was off as Moderator of the New South Wales Synod of the Uniting Church, meeting old friends and again preaching to large congregations, though nothing like earlier occasions. I got the rare opportunity of going with a group from the Church to Alice Springs. The occasion was the 25th Anniversary of the opening of the wonderful John Flynn Memorial Church. We were led by a truly great man and splendid friend, the Very Rev. Fred McKay, who succeeded the famous John Flynn as leader of the Australia Inland Mission. From Alice we went first to a cattle station several miles out, Bond Springs. That day they had been rounding up the cattle, first by flying a light aircraft hither and yon, gradually gathering them in from their wide dispersal, when the horsemen took over. There they were in the stockyards, looking in prime condition, though what they fed on one could not imagine. It must have been profitable, for the cattle station had every luxury, including a swimming pool, and the owner's wife, by the verdict of the ladies of our party, though informally dressed, was 'dripping with diamonds' – and I never noticed! From there to the grave of John Flynn, a huge round boulder. Young vandals had recently sprayed it with aerosol paint, and the only way to get it off was to sand blast it. We flew from Alice to Ayers Rock and the Olgas – a splendid way to view these geological marvels. We were lucky with our guide to the Rock, who was a geology lecturer. Someone asked him:

'Is it the case that the Rock is like an iceberg, with one eighth above ground, and seven below?'

'Who told you that nonsense? There are about 1,100 feet above, and some 25,000 below.'

The Rock is marvellous the way it changes colour, in different conditions of light, from sunrise to sunset. We also did a two-day safari, taking in all the gorges in the Macdonnel Ranges, including Simpson's Gap, cut sheer through, and so orientated that the sun shines direct down at noon on midsummer's day. We also visited the Harrisonburg Mission for Aborigines, set up over a century ago by Lutheran monks, who set out from Adelaide with flocks and herds and arrived two years later. We drove along the dry bed of the Finke River, one of the oldest in the world, just dry sand so deep even the 4-wheel-drive safari truck stuck hopelessly, yet the brushwood was clinging three feet up on the trees, showing the level of the last flood. We finished up with a picnic round the fire after dark, and sang the 23rd Psalm to Crimond.

I went back again during the vacancy when Graham retired; also a Long Service leave in Killara, and was at Adelaide and Perth again. I started a new line with three months in a vacancy in St. Andrew's, Canberra, with two subsequent visits. Every time I also went to Scots, Melbourne, till they asked me to stop saying this was my farewell visit – I was getting as bad as Nellie Melba with her farewell concerts!

Mention of these latest visits to the Churches named, St. Andrew's, Canberra, and Scots, Melbourne, reminds me that they are the two remaining literal strongholds of what I usually describe as 'main stream Presbyterianism', among the sad things that are happening in the Continuing Presbyterian Church in Australia. I have already mentioned in connection with Scot's, Melbourne, the bitterness caused by the badly bungled Union with the Methodist and the Congregational Churches. Since then

things have gone from bad to worse. Many Presbyterians who went into the
Uniting Church with high hopes have been disappointed and disillusioned.
The Presbyterian Church itself has more and more been 'taken over' by
groups with a very narrow 'right wing' attitude. They are anti-ecumenical
and ultra-fundamentalist. Their ranks have been augmented by an assort-
ment of people with no Presbyterian background. It is typical that when
Norman Pritchard was Moderator of the Victorian Church one Presbytery
he was due to visit debated if they would receive him, because he had said
that, although he was out of the country at the time of the Pope's visit, he
would have joined the Reception to him had he been available.

The other issue they have targeted, first in each State Assembly and then
in the General Assembly, is the Ordination of women, and they have got it
passed that the ordination of women is contrary to the Word of God and
the laws of God, and there are to be no more. I unkindly asked them what
they were going to do about the ones who were ordained already, as I knew
no liturgical formula for the un-frocking of a woman minister! It is all very
sad, and bitterly divisive. In an attempt to 'stop the rot' there was founded
recently an organisation pledged to uphold the principles of mainstream
Presbyterianism, very much as these are set out in our Preamble to
Ordination. It is called 'The Burning Bush', and I helped to launch it, by
giving the keynote address on 'Values worth preserving in Presbyterianism'.
The latest is that the narrow-minded brethren are trying to get this
organisation declared heretical!

On all these latest visits to whichever Congregation I have always stayed
with the Himmelhoch family for at least part of the time. I have now
married all three daughters and the one son, and christened six grandchildren. On three occasions I also managed over to Wellington to see Winifred
and Colin. Cumulatively, I have now lived $2\frac{1}{2}$ years in Australia.

Having lived for the long period just mentioned in that great country,
carrying out ministries of over three months on several occasions in Sydney,
Melbourne and Canberra, I must have some impressions, which I ought to
record, with reservations. It has to be remembered that I was, on all these
occasions, leading a kind of 'sheltered existence', living among and dealing
with people who were reasonably well off and 'nice Churchy types'. I never
saw at first hand the kind of life that prevails, say, in the King's Cross area
of Sydney. There was a twisted conundrum that went like this: 'Why and
where does Sydney have the largest plant in the Southern Hemisphere?'
Answer: 'In the King's Cross, because it is the biggest "sinner area".'

The overwhelming impression of Australia, quite unreserved, is what a
huge country it is. We see it on one page of a school atlas, and it looks like a

big island; it is really a continent. It takes almost as long to fly from Sydney to Perth as from Prestwick to New York. The population is unevenly distributed; if you take a pair of compasses, put the point on the south-east tip and use a radius of 750 miles, you take in fully three-quarters of the total population . . . It has huge natural resources. Sir Robert Watt, professor of agriculture at Sydney University, son of a Stewarton farmer, and brother of Professor Hugh Watt of New College, told me you could divide the country into three parts – one third already developed, one third being developed, and another third that could grow anything, if only you could get water there. Its history is still important; early on, one didn't dare mention convicts; now it is becoming almost a status symbol to have convict ancestors, like the Daughters of the American Revolution!

Most significant is the part played from the beginning, and still being played, by Scots. I mentioned the Scots concert in Brisbane; Governor Brisbane came from Largs, and Governor McQuarrie of Sydney from Mull. I had to propose the toast of The Old Scotch Collegians in Melbourne, in other words the former pupils of Scotch College; I came up with a list of 200 Scots who had played or were playing a leading part in the life of Australia. The Governor General when I was in Canberra was a Watsonian, Sir Ninian Stephen. On the other hand recent years have seen a great influx of 'new Australians' of many races, cultures and religions. Those from the Balkan States take their ancient feuds with them, and have to be searched for weapons at the soccer grounds. The Turks tend to create special problems; the women have lived in a sort of semi-purdah; they make little attempt to learn English, and form a kind of ghetto which can breed crime and delinquency. The Roman Catholic population has been boosted by immigrants from Spain and Italy; the Chinese are very industrious, and the Greeks normally do well, mainly in the catering trade. This heterogeneous influx, allied to the attitude of many of the younger generation, has led to a swing away from the old affinity to Britain as the Mother Country. An anti-Royalist and pro-republican attitude is more common.

Politically there are large problems. We were in Melbourne at the time of the constitutional crisis, when Sir John Kerr, the Governor General, dismissed Gough Whitlam, the Labour Prime Minister, over the impasse caused when the Lower House presented a budget which the Upper House refused to sanction. There were some unpleasant reactions. There was a dinner in the Masonic Hall at which Sir John was present; the 'rent a mob' crowd of demonstrators were out in full force, putting marbles under the police horses to make them fall. There was a dance near the Colvins' home; the same kind of mob were there, spitting on the ladies' dresses. Some time later, when I was in Canberra, there was what Paul would have called 'spiritual wickedness in high places'. A woman senator took her lesbian partner to a conference in Hong Kong and charged her expenses as her 'spouse'. Two years ago, when planning the programme for the official opening of the new Parliament House, the Prime Minister Bob Hawke, son of a Congregational minister but a declared agnostic, decided that in their country where so many held different faiths or, like himself, held none, they would not bother having a prayer. He submitted the proposed programme, and got back a short answer: 'No prayer – no Queen.'

In spite of these, and many economic problems, Australia remains a great country, with its yet undeveloped potential, its wonderful facilities for sport and the open air life. We have to remember that there is no such thing as a typical Australian, any more than there is a typical Scot. The ones I have met are kind and gracious people, and splendid friends whom it was a joy to meet, and I apologise to them for still insisting that I am glad I live in Scotland.

Another process started when the Minister of Portobello Old and Windsor Place persuaded me to act as interim moderator and locum in the vacancy caused by his departure to Killearn. So for six months I commuted between my home and Portobello, and enjoyed it thoroughly. It was so much more satisfying than doing what I call 'butterfly preaching', going to some special anniversary in a strange Church, among folk you never saw before, and will never see again. This was sharing the lives of the people, getting to know them, building up a relationship. Since then I have done a similar locumship in Ratho, Mayfield (short term), Davidson's Mains, St. Stephen's, Comely Bank, and I have just finished in Fairmilehead for the second time in two years. I also fill in during the summer in my own home congregation of Greenbank.

But the longest and most memorable was in St. Columba's, Pont Street, London, when Fraser McLuskey was off as Moderator. It was a great experience to share for nine months the life of that very special congregation, its varied activities, its peculiar function as a centre of Scottish life and worship, a blessed home from home, especially for young exiled Scots. I happened to be there at the Centenary Service of the Church on that site. The previous building had been burned down by enemy action one Saturday night in 1941, and this splendid new Church had risen from the ashes after the War. I had attended the old Church back in 1920, when the Scottish Scouts at the first World Jamboree paraded to St. Columba's, and sat in the pew marked Lord Rowallan (he later became Chief Scout). Her Majesty the Queen was at the Centenary Service at her own suggestion – her

Mother had laid the foundation stone of the new Church. This produced a strange situation. Fraser was there as Moderator to convey the greetings of the General Assembly, so he could not also be the local Minister, and I had to welcome Her Majesty, then welcome him to his own Church. I was happily able to function as one of Her Majesty's Chaplains in Scotland.

Apart from such locums I did a short Mission in Bermuda. The Island has 55,000 inhabitants, 60% black, a parliament, a Governor-General, and ninety-two different sects or denominations! Twenty-eight of them, after two years of arguing, had agreed on a Bible Conference – I was the white speaker. I went to the Opening Rally and was scared stiff – everyone jumping up, crying: 'Praise the Lord! Hallelujah! Thank you, Jesus!' I panicked . . . this is not my cup of tea, how can I get out of this? However, all went well. We took in five denominations each evening; the hot gospellers cooled down; the ordinary folk hotted up. The singing was terrific, and the enthusiasm uplifting – altogether a tremendous experience, if not quite like St. Cuthbert's!

As well as these two successions of interesting extra opportunities, I have had time to continue some long-standing activities, and become involved in a few new ones. I mentioned earlier my twenty-five years as Chaplain to James Gillespie's High School for Girls. I had to give that up when it changed its character, but a similar relationship still continues with St. Denis School. The boarders used to attend St. Cuthbert's, and I became ex-officio School Chaplain, and also for many years a governor. St. Denis is now amalgamated with Cranley, but I still function after thirty-six years – I am now teaching the grand-daughters of some of my first pupils! I include among what I call my old girls, well-known people like Hannah Gordon. On chaplaincies, though in a different area, I have been for twenty-five years Chaplain to the Co-optimist Rugby Club; between that and the connections of Ronald and Colin with Watsonians, as players and officials (Colin is the Club doctor), and Catriona's husband, Graham Young, having played for Scotland against Wales, and now being a SRU selector, I have connections in the right places.

Another Chaplaincy, which had lasted longer than any, finally came to an end in 1991. That year the Air Training Corps celebrated the 50th Anniversary of its Founding in February 1941; I had been Chaplain to the Kilmarnock Squadron from the start, and Regional Chaplain from 1953, so decided to call it a day. Including the Special Anniversary Services I had taken part in three Services in St. Clement Dane's, and three in St. Giles', and very recently shared in the ceremonial handing over of a Memorial

Plaque to St. Giles', commemorating these three occasions. I was very happily succeeded by the Very Rev. John M. K. Paterson, who had served in the RAF during the War. As a final fling they took me up in a powered glider from Kinloss!

Apart from references during our Cramond years, I have said little about ventures into the world of radio and TV; over the years these were fairly frequent – some occasions stand out. We did a Communion Service from St. Cuthbert's for the BBC, all very carefully timed. Using the twenty-eight silver cups, including the four originals from 1619, from which all the others have been copied, we managed to serve 1,200 communicants in fifteen minutes. Shortly after, I had a phone message from Father Quinn, a priest on the staff of the Church of the Sacred Heart in Lauriston, saying that he had finished his own duties by 10.00 a.m. that Sunday and had watched the Service on TV. 'That was the first time I had seen a Protestant Communion Service, and you may be interested to hear my impressions. First . . . I was impressed and moved by the dignity and beauty of the Service, and second, . . . a child could understand what was happening.' Interesting indeed.

On Epiphany Sunday another year we did a Service for the ITV Network, and I got the chance of doing something I had long dreamed of doing – putting on a modern version of the story of the Three Wise Men. The First was a black student from Biafra, who was studying at the Dick Vet, and was, in fact a Roman Catholic. He brought forward and laid in front of the Communion Table his microscope, and said a prayer, dedicating the skills he was learning to the service of his country. The Second was an Arab from Dar-es-Salaam; he had been in a concentration camp because his brother had been involved in an unsuccessful coup; in the camp he had come across a New Testament in Swahili, left by a Red Cross worker; purely on the strength of reading that book, when he came out he was baptised, and was now studying at the BTI in Glasgow, to go out to Aden; he brought out the book that had led him to Christ. The Third was a beautiful Tibetan woman, headmistress of a school at Kalimpong, doing a special course at Moray House; she brought a lovely picture of the Himalayas, the top part oil paint, the foreground embroidered with flowers of these famous mountains. It was most impressive.

I also did a series of lectures on the Apostles' Creed. They were staged in our large Hall, thirty minutes each, with question sessions. These were later published under the title 'What I believe'. Unfortunately the St. Andrew Press let them go out of print after two editions; several ministers used them as a handbook for Communicants' Classes.

It may be appropriate at this stage to refer to the few books I have produced. I did the Warrack Lectures on Preaching in 1959; these were published under the title *With Ardor and Accuracy*. In the series 'The Scholar as Preacher' I produced two books of sermons – *No Uncertain Sound* and *No Other Name*. In addition, when we were in Cramond there was privately produced *The Problem of Suffering* . . . Studies in the Book of Job.

Because of Jean's illness I became Chairman of the Edinburgh Branch of The Parkinson's Disease Society. We arrange meetings during the winter months for our 200 members, for entertainment, instruction and fellowship. The Rotary Club kindly supply drivers for the more disabled. Recently we have been able to set up in the Royal Victoria Hospital an Assessment Clinic for PD patients, where a doctor and nurse have ample time to study each individual case, as a busy GP with a crowded waiting-room has not. This sponsored activity has been made possible mainly by a large legacy from Miss Jean K. Bertram, who was deputy head of George Watson's Ladies College. Jean Bertram was my partner in the North Berwick tennis team all those years ago!

Most challenging and interesting is the work of Age Concern Scotland. The late Lord Wheatley got me inveigled into being Chairman in 1980 – I did three years, then five as one of the vice-Chairmen, and am now President, though not Honorary, as I do most of their public relations work. I speak to schools, senior citizens' clubs, welfare committees and, most important, nurses or therapists in training. I have spoken upon behalf of the disadvantaged elderly in the General Assembly on several occasions, and have lobbied MPs in Westminster. This is one situation where it is a distinct advantage to be old yourself!

I have called this chapter 'The Bonus Years', for I am acutely aware how fortunate I am to have come to this stage still engaged in a vocation which I can follow, as I am privileged to do, so long after official retirement, and to be granted the health and strength of mind and body still to do so much. With the death of George McLeod I am now the senior surviving ex-Moderator of the General Assembly and find myself, more and more often, in situations where my only distinction is to have lived longer than other people. That, of course, is the basic bonus.

Looking back over a very full and varied life, one experience stands out, in a category all by itself; I mean our Ecumenical Pilgrimage to the Holy Land in 1973. It was truly ecumenical, made up of thirty Scottish Episcopal, with three canons, twenty-two Roman Catholic with Bishop Monaghan, and thirty Church of Scotland, with John Lusk and myself – my crowd

Ecumenical Holy Land Pilgrimage, outside the Dome of the Rock

maintained that one ex-Moderator was as good as a broadside of canons! The tour was very well arranged by Canon Ernest Brady, who had done fifteen such, and had all the right contacts. All through we were given to understand that if you were not episcopally confirmed, you were not quite out of the top drawer – it was never obtruded, it was just there, and none of us worried about it. We all did our own thing about celebrating Eucharist, Mass, or Communion. Anyone was free to attend or not; there was one celebration for each which all must attend. The Episcopal Eucharist was celebrated in the garden at Emmaus, the Roman Catholic Mass round the the high altar of the Church of the Transfiguration on Mount Tabor. Because of vandalism our Communion had to be moved from Tabgah on the shore of the Sea of Galilee to the Church of the Multiplication, built over the mosaic of the loaves and fishes on the site of the Feeding of the Five Thousand. It is run by German Franciscans, who happily allowed us to celebrate a Church of Scotland Communion, with four elders, two of them women! We followed the Gospel story, with a week in Jerusalem, where on Maundy Thursday we started in the Upper Room, processed to Gethsemane, and ended kneeling in prayer around the rock in the Church of All Nations, and singing 'Rock of ages'.

We spent the second week living in the Church of Scotland Hospice at Tiberias. For many of us the highlight was the visit to the Nazareth Hospital of the Edinburgh Medical Missionary Society, of which I had been a director for several years. I shall never forget the lovely Chapel, with the carpenter's bench for a Communion Table. I came away with the wonderful feeling that all through I had been walking 'In the steps of the Master'. On our last evening, Ernest Brady was making his final announcements and explained that we had to leave at 5.00 a.m. to go by special bus to Tel Aviv – obviously we could not expect the warden and his wife to give us breakfast at that ungodly hour. I got up and said:

'On the contrary, I've just been speaking to them, and they'll be delighted to give us breakfast.'

'What have you got that I haven't got?' asked Ernest.

'Church of Scotland ordination' I replied quietly.

The roof nearly came off the place! I have enjoyed that status for just over sixty years, but I have some way to go to catch up with my father, on sixty-nine, or grandfather with his phenomenal seventy-two.

On the last day of the annual holiday in Iona, that blessed Isle which has meant so much to me and mine, I used to go away in the evening, all by myself, to the West side, and sit there, looking out over the vastness of the ocean, where, as they said in that famous film *Whisky Galore*: 'There's nothing out there – chust America'. I was a laddie of seven again, at the Seaside Mission on the sands below the Manse in which the nurse announced: 'John Knox has arrived,' singing, as I did not long ago, with the children of Fairmilehead Church from Junior Praise:

> 'Wide, wide as the ocean,
> high as the heavens above;
> deep, deep as the deepest sea,
> is my Saviour's love'.

I was a Divinity student, being reassured by Grandpa McEwen, seventy-two years ordained and ninety-three years young, about an inexhaustable subject; and I was praying, as I now do, the old lines which I used as a retirement prayer: Oh, use me, Lord, use even me, Just as Thou wilt, and when and where.'